D1450270

The Corvette in the Barn

The Corvette in the Barn

More Great Stories of Automotive Archaeology

TOM COTTER

FOREWORD BY KEITH MARTIN
Publisher *Sports Car Market* and *Corvette Market* magazines

First published in 2010 by Motorbooks, an imprint of MBI Publishing Company, 400 First Avenue North, Suite 300, Minneapolis, MN 55401 USA

Motorbooks titles are also available at discounts in bulk quantity for industrial or sales-promotional use. For details write to Special Sales Manager at MBI Publishing Company, 400 First Avenue North, Suite 300, Minneapolis, MN 55401 USA.

To find out more about our books, visit us online at www.motorbooks.com.

ISBN-13: 978-0-7603- 3797-4

Editors: Lee Klancher and Darwin Holmstrom
Design Manager: Brenda C. Canales
Layout by: Diana Boger

On the cover: Bill McKinnon, who has owned the car since 1967, wasn't interested in selling, but said that he enjoyed meeting Keith and his father, Don, and that they could come visit any time they liked. *Tom Cotter*

On the back cover: This rusty relic of a Model A Ford coupe didn't attract too much attention in the junkyard because of its terrible condition, except to Ron Kester. He realized it was the very hot rod he had built when he was in high school 50 years earlier. Luckily he was able to repurchase it. *John Lee*

Printed in China

I dedicate this book to all the enthusiasts
who have purchased my previous *In the Barn* books.
If you keep reading, I'll keep writing!

Contents

ACKNOWLEDGMENTS

These books are the product of so many people. I'll attempt to thank them below:

Lee Klancher has been my editor for every book I've written. Thanks, Lee, and I hope it continues. Also, the folks at Motorbooks who treat me like family: Zack Miller, Darwin Holstrom, Nichole Schiele, and the rest of the staff, thanks.

Two friends have been involved in each *In the Barn* book: Ken Gross and Jay Leno. The fact that I even know you guys is an honor, but realizing you are actually contributors to my projects is quite humbling. In fact it was Jay who suggested I keep using the *In the Barn* name in my future books after *Cobra* was published. He convinced me that the name had a brand value that I should not drop.

And I'm thrilled that my old pal Randy Leffingwell, who I worked beside 25 years ago, contributed the great Corvette Z06 roadster story. Thank you, Randy.

And to everyone who contributed a lead, a story, or photographs to *The Corvette In the Barn*, thank you; I couldn't have done this book without you. In no particular order, a big thank you to: Bill McKinnon, Harold Pace, Steve Katzman, Geoff Hacker, Guy Dirkin, Corey Petersen, George Prentice, Bill Connell, Andy Saunders, Vince Leto, Dave Redman, Jim Kane, Daniel Strohl, Edd Ellison, Jeff Trask, Jim & Sandra McNeil, Jamie del Valle, Scott Mason, Earl Pfeifer, Kay Hottendorff, Ard op de Weegh, Arnoud op de Weegh, Don Isley, Keith Isley, Jack Walter, Alan Sangiacomo, Chris Unger, Mike Wales, Joe Troilo, Don Prudhomme, Donnie Gould, Jim Taylor, Mike Goodman, John Lee, Karl Kirchner, Jim & Elyse Barrett, George Alderman, Paul Alderman, Erich Bollman, Scott Smith, Gerry Christensen, Wolfgang Blaube, Kevin Mackay, Rob Cotter, Cliff Bieder, Mark Haas, Mark Savory, Neil Rashba, and Alan Poster.

FOREWORD

By Keith Martin,
Publisher of *Sports Car Market*
and *Corvette Market*

For some, driving to the grocery store is all about the destination and loading up the family car with bread, eggs, milk, and other necessities. For Tom Cotter, going to the store is just an excuse to look for cars.

In fact, I would guess that Tom has found more circuitous ways to get anywhere than anyone else on earth. Like a big-game tracker, he's always on the lookout for that elusive bit of chrome that can be seen through a partially open garage door or a tantalizing shape under a decrepit car cover.

With *The Corvette in the Barn*, Tom has turned his attention to that most iconic of American cars. Since 1953, more than one million Corvettes have been produced, which also means that there are unfound, undiscovered Corvettes lurking nearly everywhere.

In my day job as publisher of *Sports Car Market* and *Corvette Market* magazines, we analyze the prices that collectible cars—particularly Corvettes—make when they are brought to public auction. We also look at restoration and preservation trends; 10 years ago a perfectly restored car would have been worth more than one that was original and in good shape. Today that equation has been reversed, with collectors realizing that you can restore a car many times, but it's only original once. So original cars, especially freshly discovered ones, are in high demand.

Which makes Tom's book even more timely. As with his earlier barn-find books, he has compiled tantalizing and true tales based on firsthand experiences from automotive spelunkers. Inside this book are the kinds of stories we all like to hear about cars that have been lost and found. How they went from decades in a locked garage to becoming someone's newly freshened pride and joy. How their values went from so little that they were pushed into a corner to gather dust to becoming worth hundreds of thousands of dollars.

The most delicious finds are those of vintage pre-1984 Corvettes, which have minimal electronic systems and are relatively easy to bring back to life. The best barn find of all would be a Corvette that had some verifiable racing history, which still had some very special factory-installed competition bits, such as an oversized fuel tank or big brakes.

But every Corvette is special, especially when compared with run-of-the-mill family sedans. Every new Corvette was purchased with the expectation that it would change a life, that it could provide thrills and chills to the new owner. Owning a Corvette set the owner apart from the crowd and made the statement that this person favored stylish performance.

Which, in the end, is why there are still Corvettes out there to be found. Even the most meager, low-horsepower Corvette has a degree of desirability, which makes it worth hunting, acquiring, and trailering home.

Like all of Cotter's barn-find books, this book has inspired me to drive around my neighborhood a little more carefully, seeing if that is really a Corvette poking out from under that ragged piece of canvas behind the big oak tree down the block. And when my wife reads this introduction, she'll know why it always seems to take me an hour longer to drive to the grocery store when I go alone than it does when we are together.

INTRODUCTION

I'm surprised at how characters from one book of mine become a part of another.

When I started to write this book, I was just finishing a biography about Dean Jeffries, the great California customizer. I became intrigued with the man and the cars he built. As soon as the book was completed, I found the owners of two great Dean Jeffries' creations—the spectacular Porsche 356 Four-Cam Carrera he customized, and the Green Hornet's *Black Beauty*, which appeared weekly on television. These cars were both nearing completion as this book was going to press, so both are featured inside.

I am also writing a biography on Hall-of-Fame drag racer, "TV" Tommy Ivo. I've been intrigued with Ivo since I was a kid, and writing his biography is a real thrill. And because I've been hanging around drag strips as I conduct interviews—including the Hot Rod Reunion in Bakersfield (better known as the Cacklefest)—I uncovered a few barn-find stories about drag cars. These are the cars I grew up admiring while I was reading *Hot Rod* magazine instead of doing my homework.

I also enjoyed reading *Rod & Custom*, where the column "Vintage Tin" was my favorite in the magazine. Years later, being much older but obviously no wiser, I reconnected with barn-find cars in the British magazines *Thoroughbred & Classic Cars, Classic & Sports Car,* and *Octane.*

The truth is that I love all kinds of cars—brass era, classics, imports, hot rods, sports cars, race cars, muscle cars, drag cars—you name it. I hope you do too. In fact, I've found that the human-interest story is always more important than the type of car discovered.

I've elected to bring other voices into my books by occasionally having both professional and non-professional writers write stories about their discoveries. I feel this adds a different dimension to the books by not forcing the reader to hear only from me!

There is nothing that would make me happier than to write a new car- or motorcycle-in-the-barn book every two years, so if you have any great stories, please send them to me. Remember, a story about a great car is not as desirable to me as a great story of discovery, regardless of the type of car. So if you have a great story, drop me a line and send me a brief description and as-found photos. You just might help me fill the next *In the Barn* book.

Tom Cotter
tcotter@cobrainthebarn.com

CHAPTER ONE

Dream Cars

The Silver Dollar
in the Barn

For many enthusiasts, the seed for acquiring an old car is planted early in life. A permanent image of a certain car is burned into the hard drive of the brain, and age does not dilute that image.

Such was the case with Chris Unger, a car-crazy youth who was exposed to drag racing early in life.

"I was thirteen years old when we moved to Orange, California, and my older brother would let me tag along with him on weekends to Lyons Drag Strip in Escondido," said Unger. "Early on, I heard there was an old A-Gas Willys sitting in a barn somewhere in Escondido. It apparently belonged to an electrician who lived in the area."

Unger grew up in the heart of drag racing country during the golden era of the 1960s. Like scores of young guys during that time, he was attracted to the pure horsepower and muscle of the A- and B-Gas cars, especially the Willys gassers that were once common.

Unger had never actually seen the Willys gasser, but he had heard the rumors that it was put into storage before he moved to Orange. In his mind's eye, he knew just what it looked like. He knew it was a 1940 Willys pickup truck called the *Silver Dollar,* so he imagined it was silver in color. And like all proper gassers of the day, it probably had a straight tubular front axle and magnesium wheels.

"So eventually I found the electrician, Mike, and we became friends over the years. At one point as a young fellow, I was even an apprentice electrician for him."

Even though they had become friends, though, Mike never offered to show Unger the *Silver Dollar.*

Mike had built the Willys from a stock steel truck in 1960 and originally painted it red. According to Unger, it was featured in some early-1960s rodding magazines before some of the steel parts were substituted for fiberglass and it was painted silver. The hood came from Cal Automotive, but Mike manufactured the fiberglass fenders and pickup bed himself and actually made a fiberglass floor panel to cut the weight. Eventually he had it down to about 1,800 pounds.

"Mike actually blew the engine up at Long Beach in 1965 and brought the car back to his shop," he said. "Because he had been running a small-block Chevy, and losing against Stone, Woods & Cook and the other Chryslers, he had plans to put a Chrysler in it. Within just a couple of weeks of bringing

Chris Unger had long heard of a forgotten 1940 Willys pickup in his neighborhood but had never seen it. In its heyday, the truck burned up the quarter-mile against other notable challengers, such as the famous Stone, Woods & Cook 1941 Willys coupe. *Chris Unger collection*

the *Silver Dollar* to his shop for the engine conversion, a lady driving by lost control of her Nash and drove through his garage, hitting the Hemi engine and knocking it into the Willys. It dented the bodywork, and Mike got an insurance settlement.

"Mike was sick over the episode, so he patched up the wall of his garage and just put the *Silver Dollar* away in a barn behind his mother's house. I mean, Mike wouldn't even drive his cars in the rain, so he just felt terrible."

Even when Unger had known Mike for a couple of years, he still had never seen the Willys. That changed on one fateful day in 2008.

"I traded this 1940 Ford in 1966 or 1967 after I blew it up on the way home from a Doors concert, believe it or not" said Unger. "I traded it for an altered 1940 Ford pickup. It had a big engine in it, but it only had a 1939 Ford gearbox, so I'd scatter those transmissions after just two runs at the drag strip. Once I broke off the back of the bell housing.

"So I asked Mike if he knew how to weld cast iron. He said yes, but that we had to go out to his mother's house to get the special I-Rod for cast-iron welding. I knew this was where the *Silver Dollar* was stored."

Forty-two years after Unger heard about the Willys, he was finally able to see the car. The car had been stored in this Southern California barn in the 1960s and had never left. *Chris Unger collection*

Mike opened the garage door for the first time since the lady drove through the wall of his shop, at least two years earlier. Chris caught a glimpse of the *Silver Dollar*. He loved it and offered to buy the car on the spot. Mike declined.

But 42 years later, Mike finally relented and made the phone call Unger had been waiting so long to hear.

"He called me and asked if I was still interested in buying the *Silver Dollar*," Unger said. "He wanted to build a Dearborn Deuce roadster and wanted to sell all his stuff and invest it into his new hot rod.

"It had been down in the dirt, having been knocked off the stands a long time ago."

Unger bought the car and finally installed an engine to replace the one that had blown up in 1965. Interestingly, the only item that was missing was the unique aluminum air scoop that had protruded from the Willys hood. Unger had one fabricated to duplicate the original.

"The scoop went with the engine when the insurance company paid Mike off for the lady driving through his shop," said Unger. "The crazy thing is, I owned that scoop on my '40 Ford when I was seventeen! I must have gotten it from someone who got it from the insurance company."

Straight-front axle Willys gassers have always had an attitude. Unger has put the truck back together but refuses to restore it because that would wipe away the originality. *Chris Unger collection*

Unger has owned the Willys for a couple of years, but only got serious about getting it running again six months before the 2009 Bakersfield Hot Rod Reunion event.

"I'm not sure it's such a good idea [to make it race ready], because it's such a bitchin' relic and a survivor," he said. "You put all that power in this old truck and it could flip over and ruin it."

In the meantime, the *Silver Dollar* will be seen at certain nostalgic car shows, but will only drive around at idle speed. And its proud owner, Chris Unger, will feel like that 13-year-old kid every time he fires it up.

To Unger, it was worth the 42-year wait.

The Twisted Tale
of the Jeffries' Porsche

In 2009, I wrote a biography about California customizer Dean Jeffries (*Dean Jeffries: 50 Fabulous Years in Hot Rods, Racing & Film*, Motorbooks 2009). One of Jeffries' most significant custom creations was a Porsche Carrera that he customized as a young man when he rented space behind George Barris' shop.

The rare sports car was molded into an appealing shape and featured non-traditional headlights, taillights, and scoops. And it was painted pearl silver. Jeffries speaks proudly that even though it was frowned on to customize sports cars—especially Porsches in the 1950s and 1960s—his Carrera was universally appreciated by enthusiasts and even got a "thumbs-up" from a Porsche factory representative. The car was featured on the cover of the October 1959 issue of *Rod & Custom* magazine.

One day a man walked into Jeffries' Hollywood, California, shop and said he wanted to buy the Porsche that was sitting outside. "That's fine and dandy," Jeffries told him. "But I want all cash."

The man said, "Fine, because that's all I deal with."

Jeffries didn't know that the man was wanted for murder and bank robbery. He paid cash for the car and, as Jeffries said, "Drove down the road."

To this day Jeffries regrets selling the Porsche and has said for many years that he would love to buy it back to add to his small collection.

The man, Albert Nussbaum, apparently drove the car from Southern California to his sister's house near Fort Lauderdale, Florida, trying to avoid the police. Ultimately he was arrested, and the car remained in his sister's driveway for two to three years.

The Porsche disappeared until 1964, when it reappeared briefly repainted in white. The rare and temperamental four-cam Carrera engine had been removed, and a standard pushrod Porsche motor had been installed in its place.

Amelia Island Concours d'Elegance founder and co-chairman Bill Warner followed up rumors that the car still existed somewhere on the East Coast. He found the owner and made arrangements to bring it to the 2009 Concours for Jeffries to see for the first time in nearly 50 years.

As Jeffries walked around the car, which was halfway through a restoration, he had tears in his eyes.

How had such a famous car gone undiscovered for so many decades? Jack Walter knows.

Walter was your average car-crazy teen in 1971. He had just graduated from high school and was eager to own a Porsche.

When Jack Walter bought this intriguing Porsche in the 1970s, he just liked the look. He didn't know that it left the factory with a four-cam Carerra engine, that famous California customizer Dean Jeffries had customized it, or that it had been featured on the cover of magazines decades earlier. *Jack Walter*

"I had been a Porsche nut from an early age," said Walter, 58, of Atlanta. "When I was fourteen years old I read a 1966 *Car & Driver* story about a black Porsche Speedster called *Ode to a Bathtub*. It left a huge impression on me."

Upon graduation, Walter went searching for a Speedster of his own. He saw an advertisement for one being sold by Atlanta-based race driver Jim Downing, who at the time had a little shop.

"It was painted with primer and he was asking six hundred dollars for it," said Walter. "I only had four hundred dollars, so I brought my dad along hoping I could borrow the extra two hundred dollars. But he just saw this old Speedster and wouldn't loan me the money."

Walter's father hoped to satisfy his son's desire for a sporty convertible by buying him a Corvair Corsa Turbo convertible for $275. The car had a dropped valve, so his dad wanted him to invest some "sweat equity" into the car before it could become roadworthy.

"I rebuilt the engine and had it balanced," he said. "I had it up to two hundred forty horsepower."

Still, as cool as it was, the hot little Corvair failed to satisfy the young Walter's desire for a Porsche.

When Jeffries' pinstriping, painting, and customizing career was just starting out in the 1950s, he used this car as his calling card at car shows. He originally painted the car pearl silver, then painted it pearl gold (as shown), then painted it silver again before selling it to a "killer and a bank robber." *Jack Walter collection*

Walter used to hang out at a friend's house whose older sister, Peggy Dale, was a sports car enthusiast; she owned a Fiat Spyder. Her mechanic, Sandy, found a strange-looking Porsche coupe while on a Florida trip in 1969, so he bought it and towed it home.

As soon as she saw it, Peggy wanted to own the Porsche, but Sandy wasn't interested in selling it. But her mechanic friend had a gambling problem and called Peggy to borrow some money to pay off the "leg-breakers" who were on their way over to his house.

"No, I won't loan you money, but I will buy your Porsche," said Peggy, who at the time was 24 years old. Even though he had wanted more money for the car, Sandy accepted $1,100 because he had recently crashed the car into the back of a truck and it sustained some body damage.

Peggy bought the car and Walter remembers the first time he saw it while he was over visiting Peggy's brother.

"I saw it at her parent's home and I made three laps around the car before I walked into the house," he said. "Sell me the car," he said to Peggy.

She ignored him, proud of her new set of wheels.

Walter said that Peggy used the Porsche every day. She lived near a downtown Atlanta bar, so unfortunately she parked the unique car in the streets. Every time Walter saw her he would ask, "When are you going to sell me the car?"

In 1971, Peggy told Walter she was trying to raise money so she could travel to Katmandu. "I'll sell you the car for what I paid, one thousand one hundred dollars," she said.

"I said, 'OK!'" said Walter.

He drove the car home. Immediately his father asked why he bought the beat-up Porsche.

Walter said the registration slip identified the car as a Sebring coupe, but he really thought the car was just a local Florida custom. He began saving to get the damaged nose repaired.

As he investigated his new purchase, he began to notice some unusual features; the Porsche had two switches next to the steering wheel for the coils. It also appeared that the car once housed a dry-sump oiling engine, as was typical in racing Porsches.

About this same time—1971 or 1972—Walter said that he saw an ad in *AutoWeek* magazine asking for photos and information on a custom Porsche that was built by Dean Jeffries in the late 1950s.

"I still didn't know I owned Dean Jeffries' Porsche, but I certainly knew who Dean Jeffries was," said Walter. "He built the Monkeemobile and the Kyote Dune Buggies. I always wanted one of those dune buggies."

Eventually he got the Porsche's nose repaired "with lots of Bondo," and started to drive the Porsche quite a bit, even though he still owned his Turbo Corvair.

"So I sent photos of my car to the guy who advertised in *AutoWeek*," he said. "I wrote, 'Is this what you're looking for?'

"I got back a six-page letter with copies of magazine articles and a letter from the man. He said he had seen it at a car show in the 1950s."

Finally he knew what he owned.

Walter joined the Atlanta Region of the Porsche Club of America, but when he wrote on his application that he had a customized Porsche, they gave him a bad time. That is, until he told them it was the Dean Jeffries' Porsche; then members started telling him that Jeffries actually enhanced the car's original lines.

"I couldn't believe I own this car," he said. "I actually built Dean Jeffries model cars when I was a kid. I was so excited."

In 1973, a friend of Walter's who owned a Porsche 550 Spyder suggested that he consider purchasing a proper four-cam engine for the Jeffries Porsche.

"He knew a guy in Jacksonville who had three Carrera engines, so I said,

Dean Jeffries was reunited with the partially restored Porsche after nearly 50 years at the 2008 Amelia Island Concours d'Elegance in Florida. Jeffries will come to Amelia again to see the finished product when it is completed. *Jack Walter*

'OK, let's get one,'" said Walter. "We drove down in his friend's new Honda Civic hatchback and picked up the engine. I paid nine hundred dollars."

Walter tells a funny tale of driving back to Atlanta in the Honda with the four-cam engine in clear view through the large hatchback window.

"A Porsche comes blasting past us in the fast lane, then slams on its brakes when the driver saw the engine we were hauling," said Walter. "It turns out it was [Porsche race driver] Hurley Haywood, who just wanted to see it."

In 1974, Walter painted the Porsche white with a dark blue GT40-type stripe that ran from front to rear. (It was in this configuration that *Rod & Custom* ran a photo of the car in 1990.)

Then the car went into a 20-year hibernation.

Walter was in a funk. He had too many cars and not enough time.

"A friend of mine said he walked into his garage when he turned fifty years old and realized that he'd have to live to one hundred in order to finish all his car projects," said Walter. "He sold off a bunch of projects and used the money to fix up his favorites.

"It took me a couple of years to come to the same conclusion. I had a Porsche sunroof coupe—six hundred forty serial numbers after the Carrera—that I sold. I sold a BMW 2002tii as well."

His new goal was to restore the Porsche he had owned since 1971.

"I want to bring the Porsche to display at Amelia Island restored to the exact way it looked when it rolled out of Dean Jeffries' shop in 1957," he said.

He has located a restoration shop that is doing an exquisite job on the body, and he will have the interior duplicated.

But the restoration is expensive, certainly more than his job at Lockheed can comfortably afford. Luckily Bill Warner from Amelia Island talked paint sponsor BASF into donating the paint for the project. And Dean Jeffries himself sat down with a company rep to ensure the color and the metallic flake would be just right.

"Dean Jeffries said he'd like to buy it back, and I said I'd trade it for his GT40," said Walter.

"I'm just an engineer and can't really afford to own a car that valuable. When the car is done, I might just let it go to a Porsche collector with deep pockets.

"A standard Carrera coupe is worth three hundred thousand to five hundred thousand dollars these days. Certainly this one is more valuable. At least it might allow me to retire a little bit early."

Sniping a Mustang
Prototype

One night in 2005, Mark Haas was doing what many of us do each evening: checking the eBay listings for interesting cars and parts. For Haas, the ritual includes searching on his favorite topic: Ford. Haas is predisposed to Fords. Particularly Mustangs.

"I've been collecting cars for thirty-five years," said the 51-year-old Detroit-area native. "When I was a kid, my neighbor across the street was an Indy car team owner, so that's where I got my feet wet."

Haas' collection has a number of Mustangs, including a rare Super Cobra Jet now in restoration—and has owned a number of Boss 302s—but his specialty is SVO Mustangs. He owns eight of them.

"I've basically dedicated my life to restoring Mustangs," he said.

Not that he hasn't gotten his feet wet on other brands; Haas once drove all the way from Detroit to Arizona to buy a two-stroke, three-cylinder Saab Sonnet he heard was for sale. He fell in love with the car's odd styling.

In 2005, as he was checking out Mustang listings, he came across an older Mustang that captured his attention. The car was listed as a 1964 and had a custom front end. It was a seven-day auction, but five days into the auction, not a single bid had been placed.

The car resembled the early Mustang show car Haas remembers seeing in magazines when the car was introduced. It was the styling that attracted Haas' eye.

The Mustang was the most anticipated new car launch in history. And sales of new Mustangs surged after nearly every media outlet in the country covered the introduction.

(As a car-crazy kid born in the mid-1950s, I couldn't wait for the Mustang to be introduced. I was in fifth grade at Nokomis Elementary School in Holbrook, Long Island, New York. One day, two new Mustangs showed up in the school parking lot; the black convertible belonged to a sixth grade teacher and the green coupe belonged to the school's janitor. They had both received their new cars on the same day, and it was such an exciting event that classes were allowed to go into the parking lot, accompanied by their teachers, of course, to see the new cars. This was the most exciting moment for this young car enthusiast and a wonderful memory I still have today, more than four decades later.)

"I didn't know the Mustang was being chatted up on Ford websites and chatrooms," said Haas. "People were pooh-poohing it as a clone."

Mark Haas proudly posed next to his dream Mustang prototype at the Owls Head Museum in Maine. A few years later, he owned the sister car! Ford built several of these prototypes to display at auto shows and the New York World's Fair during the launch of the Mustang in 1964. *Mark Haas collection*

Haas went into this purchase virtually blind, led only by his enthusiasm for the stylish car. How could he go wrong? It had only 10,661 miles on the odometer, and besides, his inclinations hadn't let him down with past purchases.

During the last few moments of the auction, a bid was placed by someone for $10,000. Haas followed his heart, and without ever seeing the car in person, placed a last-minute bid (in eBay lingo, a "snipe") of $10,100 for the Mustang. He won the auction and owned the car.

Within minutes of the end of the auction, the losing bidder emailed Haas and asked if he'd like to sell the car. It was only then that Haas thought he might have stumbled onto something really special.

Haas hooked up his trailer and drove to New Jersey to pick up his new purchase.

"I bought the car from the son of an old man who had owned it since 1978," said Haas. The son told him his father was in the van-conversion business, which was a hot industry during the "If this van's a rockin', don't bother knockin'" 1970s.

The man bought stock vans for significantly lower prices in Canada. But he had to buy a truck load of vans at a time to get the discount.

The Mustang Haas bought off of eBay (!) is virtually identical to the Owls Head car, including the lift-off hardtop roof and hand-fabricated suspension and chassis components. The car features chrome-plated engine block, heads, exhaust manifolds, and steering column. *Mark Haas*

"He bought a bunch of vans, but he needed to buy one more vehicle in order to get the special pricing," said Haas. "So he bought this old Mustang that was on the dealer lot because it was cheap."

It appears that what Haas bought was an early Mustang prototype, a car that was used to make last-minute design changes before going into production. Haas calls it a pre-production buck.

"This car has a one-inch longer wheelbase than conventional Mustangs," he said. "That's because it was based on a Falcon platform. The frame has been torch cut in places to give clearance for Mustang fourteen-inch wheels instead of the Falcon's thirteen-inch wheels.

"Also, the car appears to have been converted from a coupe into a convertible. But significant reinforcement has been added to the floorpan for strength. And it has a removable hardtop."

Ford used the 1964–1965 New York World's Fair to give their new Mustang exposure to millions of consumers. Haas believes his Mustang may have been one of the prototypes displayed there.

"The VIN number in the windshield wasn't legible, but once we started to pull off the front fenders, I was able to verify the car's build date," he said. "The VIN tells me the car was built on April 20, 1964, had a 260 V-8, three-speed transmission, and a 3.0 rear axle ratio.

"But the car doesn't have a 260 in it, but has a chrome-plated 289; the engine block is actually chrome-plated, as are the cylinder heads, exhaust manifolds, and steering column. It was obviously built for display.

"But the original transmission and rear end are in the car, and each still wear production tags marked April 1964."

Haas said the car also features a 1965 Pony-type interior.

And the roof is one inch taller than on stock Mustangs.

"There is another Mustang Prototype at the Owls Head Transportation Museum in Maine, and the windshield on it is raked more than on mine," he said. "I'm told that when Henry Ford II saw the prototype with the raked windshield, he told the designers it needed to be raised one more inch."

Haas has owned the Mustang for at least five years, but virtually nobody knows of it. "Everyone is out there searching for Steve McQueen's *Bullitt* Mustang, so I've just kept this one kind of quiet.

"I have friends who ask me, 'How is it that you always find all these rare and unusual cars?' The secret is that I'm always keeping my eyes open for hidden cars. And I make friends with the past owners. I've never brought or sold a car to anyone who hasn't remained my friend.

"Every car I restore gets years of devotion, and when it gets finished, it gets covered and put in the back of my garage."

But this Mustang is special, perhaps too special to be hidden in a garage for the rest of its life.

"There are more LS6 Chevelle convertibles in the world now than GM ever built," he said. "There are a lot of fabricated cars out there, so this one is extra special because it's real.

"I'm a good buyer and a bad seller," he said. "But I can see this car becoming part of someone's collection that specializes in Mustangs or prototypes."

Perhaps Haas will sell the car on eBay.

The Enterprising Priest and His Bubble-Screened Boondoggle

Anthony Alfred Juliano prayed he was making the right decision. The young man from Philadelphia was an enthusiast of cars and airplanes and had a knack for drawing.

In 1938, someone at General Motors was shown Juliano's car sketches. They were impressed enough with the 18-year-old lad's work to offer him enrollment in Harley Earl's newly opened school for automotive design students. GM's offer came just too late; Juliano had just decided to enter the priesthood.

Torn between two loves, Juliano was committed to becoming a man of the cloth.

Father Juliano attended the Holy Ghost seminary in Philadelphia from 1934 to 1940. He became ordained a priest in 1946, one year before graduating from Ferndale in Connecticut with dual degrees; a bachelor of arts and a degree in divinity. He joined the order of the Holy Ghost Fathers and began teaching at the Virginia Military Academy. Later he became an art professor at Duquesne University in Pittsburgh.

In an attempt to get his doctorate in art and aerodynamics from Yale, Juliano was transferred to St. Mary's in Branford, Connecticut, where he was assistant pastor.

Even as Father Juliano was reading the Bible and preparing for his doctorate, he was also reading technical manuals, *Mechanix Illustrated*, and every car magazine he could get his hands on.

As he pored over magazines and manuals, he thought about how to create the safest car on the road.

"He wanted to build the safest car in the world for his parishioners," said Andy Saunders, an auto restorer and custom car builder from Poole, England, and an authority on Father Juliano. Saunders owns the Juliano-built Aurora, seen on these pages.

"His thinking was so far ahead of his time. He was a genius."

As opposed to today, where Volvo and Mercedes advertisements shout their companies' crash-test results as a marketing strategy, it was Juliano's belief that people cared more about style than safety.

Americans "won't pay for safety," he was quoted in a 1955 interview with Connecticut's *New Haven Register*. He sought to build a car that combined

Father Anthony Alfred Juliano created quite a stir as he drove the Aurora to its press introduction at the Hotel New Yorker on 35th Street in 1957. The trip from Connecticut was plagued with mechanical breakdowns, and the 90-minute drive took nearly 11 hours. *Associated Press*

"unity and originality of design," that would have consumers flocking to buy his car for its beauty and acquiring the safety benefits as a bonus.

As can be seen from the accompanying photos of the Aurora, beauty is indeed in the eye of the beholder. Nonetheless, Father Juliano surged forward with his plans.

Selling the idea of car design to his superiors on the basis that it aided his thesis studies, he set up shop in an old horse stable in Branford and bought a wrecked 1953 Buick Roadmaster. He stripped the Buick's sheet metal, straightened the mangled frame, and spent the next four years designing and tinkering on what he hoped would be the safest, most beautiful car ever built. The Aurora was named for his young niece, Dawn; *aurora* is Latin for "dawn."

"Uncle Al was a part of our household during every holiday," said Father Juliano's niece Dawn O'Mara. "I can tell you that he definitely was not a hot rodder. He didn't know anything about the mechanical parts of cars. He was more of an artist and loved to paint in oil."

He began by building a clay scale model of his design, then used plywood and fiberglass to construct a body mold. According to O'Mara, her uncle worked with Owens/Corning in the development of the Aurora's body. The roof and gullwing-type window canopy was constructed of shatterproof resin.

Father Juliano worked tirelessly on the car, aided by sympathetic parishioners and a team of teenage boys eager to get their hands dirty working on cars.

Despite the Aurora's ungainly appearance, Father Juliano designed safety features into his car that were decades ahead of the automotive industry. Starting with the passenger compartment, one of the most obvious features is the car's bubble windshield. Father Juliano specified it be made of shatterproof resin so that it would be difficult for passengers to hit their heads on the windshield, a common injury at the time. Seat belts were also built into the car's design. He mounted the car's four "captain's chairs" high and toward the center of the car in order to give better protection in the event of a side impact. The four seats were also pedestal-mounted, allowing occupants to rotate up to 360 degrees prior to a crash for better protection.

The Aurora interior also featured a race car–type roll cage made of stainless steel, recessed gauges, and eight inches of padding on the dashboard. The car featured a collapsible steering column and side-impact protection bars.

The Aurora's exterior featured a front end with a huge foam-filled crush-zone that doubled as a "cowcatcher" to cradle errant pedestrians. The spare tire was located under the nose to assist in crash protection. Above the crush zone were six headlights, which were to be replaced with a light bar if the car were put into production.

The bubble windshield eliminated the need for windshield wipers, because like a jet plane, the car's speed would push rainwater to the sides. The Aurora also featured an automatic jacking system to aid in flat tire repair or other servicing.

Father Juliano wrote a sales brochure that claimed the Aurora was the World's Safest Car. The brochure noted that the car could be ordered with any type of powerplant: Cadillac, Lincoln, Imperial, Packard, Bugatti, or Mercedes-Benz. It also listed as options such items as fuel injection and supercharging, as well as a wide assortment of interior and exterior finishes.

The Custom Automobile Corporation of America, Father Juliano's enterprise, claimed that the Aurora's fiberglass styling was, "the most advanced in the world for a production automobile. It is built to last many years and will remain substantially the same year-in and year-out—a lifetime masterpiece of automotive engineering and design."

The promise was never fulfilled, however. The prototype cost $30,000 to construct, even though Father Juliano said he could manufacture models for $12,000 each and make a profit. But in 1957, the price was huge; even though it didn't include all the innovative safety features of the Aurora, a new Cadillac during the same period was less than $5,000.

This woman clearly wanted to learn more about the unusual Aurora safety car, so Father Juliano was only too happy to raise his gullwing door and talk with her. A crowd gathered in the background to gawk at the unusual vehicle. *Associated Press*

The unfinished car was displayed at the 1956 Hartford (Connecticut) Autorama and was featured in the event program centerfold.

In 1957, en route to a press function to introduce the car to the New York media, it broke down at least 15 times on Father Juliano and needed to be towed to seven different service stations for repairs to unclog the fuel line. Apparently the Buick on which the Aurora was based had sat idle for all the years of design and construction, causing the gas tank to rust and clog the lines. That rust caused the fuel lines to clog repeatedly.

The trip from Branford, Connecticut, to Manhattan—which should have taken 90 minutes—took nearly 11 hours. At 3:00 p.m., Father Juliano once again called, saying that he was getting the Aurora's battery recharged in Harlem.

The media that had assembled at the Hotel New Yorker for the 8:00 a.m. press conference started to dissipate, and by the time the Aurora rolled up at 4:00 p.m., few media crews remained. The Associated Press, *New York Times*, and *Bridgeport Post* covered the car's arrival, but the media neglected to cover the car's safety features and instead mocked its voyage from Connecticut.

Father Juliano's project failed to attract investors or customers, so the car sat forlorn behind a Connecticut body shop for decades before being rescued by British car customizer Andy Saunders after he saw it in a magazine. *Vince Leto*

"Dream Car Arrives from Connecticut After Nightmare of Breakdowns," read the *Times* headline. The *Bridgeport Post* wrote, "Auto Built by Priest for Safety Perils Traffic," referring to the police request that Father Juliano move his car because of the rubbernecking traffic jam it had caused on 35th Street.

The Aurora's New York debut was supposed to kick off a 120-city tour around the United States, where Father Juliano had hoped to take orders from customers. Unfortunately the Aurora's styling didn't excite the public the way Father Juliano had hoped.

Additionally, questions began to arise about the funding for Father's automotive project. The car's development was at least partially funded by parishioners of St. Mary's church, and his superiors accused him of misappropriation of church donations. Others accused Father Juliano of spending parishioner donations not only for the Aurora project, but also for himself. Church officials met with Father Juliano, and he was summarily disciplined.

Father Juliano's niece, Dawn O'Mara, has her own opinion regarding the issue of her uncle's financial worries. "There were a lot of local folks who were impressed with Uncle Al's innovative ideas on safety features," said O'Mara. "You know, the seat belts, the windshield; they all wanted to get on the bandwagon because of all the positive hype.

Because much of the car's body structure was constructed of wood, the 50 years it sat outdoors caused much of the car to disintegrate. This took years for Saunders to rebuild. *Andy Saunders*

"There was the intention of great profits."

O'Mara feels that many of the parishioners who invested their savings into the Custom Automotive Corporation's Aurora project began to have second thoughts once the shine started to wear off Father Juliano's dream. They sought their money returned or at least a way to save face.

Others suggest that General Motors was behind the accusations. These theories claim that the Aurora's safety features were so advanced that it threatened GM's own safety programs and the huge corporation's reputation. GM denied any involvement.

Regardless of blame, Father Juliano was drummed out of the Order of the Holy Ghost. He was investigated by the FBI and the Internal Revenue Service, but the investigations led nowhere.

Father Juliano compared himself to the late Preston Tucker, a manufacturer of the Torpedo, which was so advanced that he claims he was forced out of business in 1948 by the big Detroit automakers who didn't want to disturb the industry's status quo. Tucker also was accused of financial scandal, which was proved to be unfounded.

What wasn't publicized, though, was that Father Juliano had also put himself into deep personal debt financing the project to completion. He was

Saunders, who builds custom show cars for a living, says the Aurora's restoration was the toughest job he has ever done. Even with its controversial styling, the car is quite dramatic in its newly restored condition.
Andy Saunders

bankrupt, and the Aurora was given as collateral to a repair shop for unpaid repair bills. The car went through several hands before landing in a field behind McPhee's Body Shop in Cheshire, Connecticut.

Juliano went on to live in Florida before moving back to Philadelphia, where he became involved in art restoration.

According to his niece, Father Juliano worked with Sotherby's and other art auction houses on painting and gold leaf frame restoration. "He was an artist in his own right," said O'Mara. "My brothers and I still own some of Uncle Al's paintings, and they are very, very good."

O'Mara said that her uncle also planned to build another car and had sketches and plans for a new design, but he never went further than the planning stages.

In 1989, her uncle was doing art research in the Philadelphia Public Library when he suffered a massive heart attack. He was rushed to nearby Hahnemann Hospital, where he was put on life support and fell into a coma.

"The hospital didn't know who he was, because his car keys were in his pocket and his wallet was in his car in the library parking lot," she said. "My brother and I were called to identify him. Then, because my own father [Anthony Raymond Juliano] was in such bad condition, also in the hospital,

The Aurora was the dream of a Catholic priest, Father Juliano, whose desire was to build the safest car in the world. Saunders has rebuilt the Aurora as the ultimate tribute to the priest with the artistic flare.
Andy Saunders

my brother and I were asked to sign to take Uncle Al off life support." He died on March 2, 1989, and was buried in the Catholic cemetery in the Drexel Hill section of Philadelphia.

By the time Father Juliano was laid to rest, his Aurora safety car had already been resting in the field for more than 30 years. The body shop owner attempted to sell the car for $10,000 in 1978, but there were no interested parties.

An issue of the British magazine *Thoroughbred & Classic Cars* featured the Aurora in their "Discovered" section, which highlights interesting classic cars that are found by readers. The car caught the attention of one interested reader—Andy Saunders. "I'd seen that car before in an old schoolbook," he said. Saunders showed the picture to his father, who said, "That's the ugliest car I've ever seen."

Saunders, who runs a custom auto fabrication shop called Andy Saunders Kustoms, Kampers and Kars in Poole, England, has always dreamed of owning a prototype dream car. He felt this was his chance.

"I studied the picture in the magazine and saw the name of the body shop in the background and was able to read the phone number," he said. Saunders called the owner of the shop where the Aurora had now rested for at least 34 years.

"I paid one thousand five hundred dollars for it without ever seeing it in person," he said. "When it arrived in England, it was absolutely knocked. It was scrap. It was falling to pieces.

"All the door frames—the A-pillars, the B-pillars, firewall, wheel arches—they were all made of wood. Having sat in the field for so long, the water completely delaminated the wood."

But the fiberglass body was a different story. The wood would need to be fabricated and fitted piece-by-piece, meaning a tough manual labor chore for Saunders. The fiberglass had deteriorated so badly it was almost melted, according to Saunders.

"Father Juliano was so far ahead of his time, he was considered weird. But I'm convinced he was a genius. The driver sits at least four-and-a-half feet from the windshield; there had never been a car built like that."

When Saunders realized what he had bought, he became depressed. He dove in and spent virtually every night and weekend restoring, in some ways remanufacturing, the Aurora. He was able to retain the original chassis and running gear, front and rear fenders, and hood.

"Custom cars are a hobby for me," he said. "It's nothing for me to spend eighteen or nineteen hours a day working on cars. I can work 8:00 a.m. to 5:00 p.m. working on cars in my business, then work until 2:00 a.m. working on my own cars. I think they are the most exciting vehicles in the world.

"The roof structure held the whole [body] together, so we had to cut it in half to disassemble and reassemble the body," said Saunders, "or else the car would have fallen apart."

The largest challenge Saunders has faced is in replicating the unusual windshield.

"I can't get anyone to build a windshield like he [Father Juliano] did," he said. "The one we built turned yellow in five years, yet the original sat outside for more than thirty years and still was clear, but unfortunately unusable."

Saunders has copies of the original sales brochure from when the Aurora was displayed at the Hotel New Yorker in 1957, and every magazine the car was featured in, but unfortunately all the photos are in black and white. One cover photo, though, in *Motor Trend*, showed the car in black and silver, so that's how the car is finished.

"The picture looked to be 'color washed,' so I'm not quite sure of the exact colors of the Aurora," he said. "But I had nothing else to go with, and couldn't find a single chip of original paint on the car."

So far Saunders has spent US$12,000 working with aircraft manufacturers trying to copy that windshield.

"That car owes me," he said. "It's the most expensive car I've ever restored. The car cost me seventy-five to eighty thousand dollars, exclusive of the hours I've invested."

So far, Saunder's restored Aurora has been featured in a number of magazines and the prestigious Goodwood Festival of Speed in England. The Petersen Automotive Museum in Los Angeles also has granted a standing invitation for the car if it ever comes to America.

Saunders, though, doesn't pull any punches regarding his feelings for the finished product.

"I hate the bloody thing," he said. "I wish I'd never bought it.

"At least if I could register the bloody thing and drive it on the road, it would be different. But this bloody windshield!"

CHAPTER TWO

Hibernating Hot Rods

The Belly Tank Tribute

By Daniel Strohl

The next best thing to finding a historically significant hot rod would be replicating a historically significant hot rod, but Geoff Hacker had neither course of action in mind when he found and bought a P-51 belly tank in August 2008 in Temecula, California.

A long time ago, a hot rodder had started to convert the 165-gallon fuel tank into a streamlined land-speed racer by adding a Model A Ford front and rear suspension and a 60-horsepower Ford flathead V-8. But the project was abandoned unfinished and left outside to weather. As Hacker found it, the would-be racer was no more than a pile of parts clustered around a carved-up belly tank.

Neither an inventor nor an innovator, the hot rodder who started the project was simply trying to follow a tradition started more than 60 years prior by living legend Bill Burke. While in Guadalcanal during World War II, he first noticed a shipment of steel belly tanks designed to provide fuel to P-51 Mustangs on long-range flights. After measuring one of the tanks, Burke thought they would offer great aerodynamics as the body of a purpose-built dry-lakes racer. Streamliner racers like Bob Rufi and Ralph Schenck had recorded impressive speeds on the dry lakes before the war, but they used totally hand-built bodies; the belly tanks Burke discovered would greatly simplify streamliner construction. So almost immediately after returning home from the war, he picked up a surplus belly tank to transform into a ground-hugging speed machine.

Fifty years later, Hacker swung by Burke's shop in Whittier, California, while en route to Temecula. The two already knew each other through Geoff's research into Allied fiberglass cars, another of Burke's postwar ventures. Hacker showed Burke some photos of the belly tank, figuring he would get a kick out of it. Upon seeing the photos, Burke noticed how much the Temecula belly tank resembled his first belly tank. "You should replicate my old speed-record car," he suggested.

At the time, Hacker had other plans in mind for the belly tank. Burke's suggestion didn't really gain traction until after Hacker returned to Florida and took the tank to Ted Kempgens and Tom Bambard of Creative Motion Concepts north of Tampa. "I realized then that Bill is famous for many of his cars, but he is most famous for his first belly tank," Hacker said. "And to build a replica of that car would be a great way to honor him."

Rather than complete the project as a generic speed-record car, Hacker decided to re-create one of the first belly tanks ever built—Bill Burke's 60-horsepower flathead. Here it is pictured during Bonneville Speed Week in August 2009. *Geoff Hacker*

Finding Burke's original belly tank would be difficult, bordering on impossible. In 1946, he sold it sans engine to Howard Wilson and Phil Remington, who ran it one more time before the tank disappeared entirely. Hacker would have to build his creation out of the tank he had on hand.

Aided by Jim Miller at the American Hot Rod Foundation, Hacker embarked on a research expedition to dig up any and all information he could find on Burke's original belly tank. That belly tank ran just three times in 1946 (reaching speeds of 131.96 miles per hour) before being sold to fund the construction a larger and faster streamliner based on 315-gallon belly tanks that were built for P-38 Lightnings. Burke ran his first belly tank with a full-size Ford flathead V-8 mounted in the front, so Hacker's, which had already been cut for a rear-engine configuration, would have to be reconfigured.

"As we researched it, we realized there was not a lot of instruction on building the early belly tanks, because everybody moved quickly to the larger tanks," Hacker said. "So we consulted heavily with Bill on how exactly he built his."

Rather than build a tube frame, as anybody building a contemporary belly tank would, Hacker purchased a Model T frame and had Creative Motion Concepts narrow and shorten it to fit the tank's profile, just as Burke once did. The 60-horsepower V-8 went by the wayside in favor of a larger 100-horsepower flathead V-8, equipped with Fenton heads and a Fenton intake. The block and heads are technically incorrect—the block dates from 1949 to 1953, several

Collector Geoff Hacker bought this unfinished belly tank lakester. The 165-gallon P-51 fighter fuel tank was discovered by Anthony Migliori and his son (pictured) and then sold to Hacker. *Geoff Hacker*

years after Burke built his first belly tank—and it was originally equipped with Edelbrock and Thickstun speed parts. But Hacker said the engine at least looked the part.

A 1937 Lincoln three-speed transmission and shortened torque tube backed the flathead, and Hacker used Model A front and rear axles and springs and 1934 Ford 17-inch wire wheels. Just as Burke had, Hacker maintained the mechanical rear brakes and ditched the front brakes. With no room for a proper seat—Burke originally welded a bicycle seat to the torque tube—Hacker researched a similar seat design. Burke originally cut down the butterfly steering wheel from a Crosley sedan, so Hacker sourced and cut down a similar wheel.

In the spring of 2009, Hacker, along with car builders Kempgens and Bambard, decided to finish the car in time for Bonneville, just 90 days away. During that time, the car builders reconfigured the tank, shaped new steel for the fairings around the engine and the cockpit, somehow found a way to fit everything into the limitations of the tank, then painted it yellow with fighter plane nose art.

Even though it didn't make any official runs at Bonneville, the belly tank still made a splash on the salt before Hacker made one more stop with it before returning to Florida—Burke's shop, a little more than a year after the original builder suggested replicating his first belly tank.

"Bill was very excited, very pleased, and very honored," Hacker said. "I just couldn't get him to stop looking at the car, and all of his neighbors poured out of their shops to see it because they had always heard about that tank, but had never seen it. I think Bill was very happy to see this car and be able to pull up those memories of the car that he built."

The Penny Saver Deuce Coupe

by Ken Gross

ook closely at this faded black-and-white photo of a hot-rodded 1932 Ford three-window coupe, which was taken in the 1950s, probably by the car's proud owner. You can see his shadow in the foreground on that sunny day long ago. The car sits in front of an alley on Somerville Street in Philadelphia. A pharmacy sign behind it reads, "Lev's Cut Rate Drugs." Nothing fancy here: scuffed rear whitewalls, blackwall tires in front, a straight front axle, no hood, not even a filled grille shell.

Compared with nearly anything else on the road in that era, this coupe was low and menacing, with that nasty outlaw look that retro rodders try so hard to mimic today. And with three Stromberg 97s atop a "full house" OHV Cadillac mill, with tubular headers, set back nearly a foot, it must have been really fast. Un-chopped, with its body channeled the full width of the frame, this fierce little deuce terrorized the streets of Philadelphia in the early 1950s.

Nearly 50 years later, the venerable three-window still bears its faded purple paint. The big OHV motor has been replaced with a 331ci Cadillac, but the 1937 Cad/LaSalle gearbox is still in place, hooked to a 1940 Ford torque-tube driveline. After all these years, the three-window retains its straight front axle, but its grille shell has been filled. Inside, Stewart-Warner convex lens gauges remain, with a couple of empty holes where precious dials were removed. The red and white vinyl door panels and brown pleated seat are cracked and stiff with age.

But they're still there.

Not unexpectedly, there's some surface rust. The rear wheels have been reversed to accommodate wider tires, and now there are cycle fenders in front. But the Guide headlights are still there, perched on accessory light stands. Even the rumble seat grab rails are intact. Over time, someone filled the lower rear panel, replacing the 1949 Pontiac taillights with lights pirated from a 1941 Chevy. Maybe that same guy was responsible for the Perfect Circle, Hildebrandt, and Schiefer decals on the passenger-side window. And did he also paint the crude "Deuces Wilde" (sic) script on the deck lid? Who knows?

When the coupe's present owner, Gerard Christensen of Scotch Plains, New Jersey, found the old hot rod from an ad in a local "penny saver" newspaper, it was located in Ventnor, New Jersey, about 100 miles from his home. The coupe had languished in dead storage for over 30 years. It had never traveled

Along with his new purchase, Gerard Christensen received some paperwork and this photograph of the car taken in the 1950s somewhere in Philadelphia. The car had a 331 Cadillac engine, Cad/Lasalle transmission, and rolled and pleated interior. *Girard Christensen collection*

far from Philadelphia. And it emerged from its garage about as you see it. A remarkable survivor, this time warp coupe resembled a page out of A.B. Shuman's wonderful book on East Coast hot rodding, *Cool Cars and Square Roll Bars.*

"When I saw the picture in the paper," Christensen says, "I raced down there and took a look. I'd just bought my wife a new Jeep so I was short of cash. Luckily, the owner was into bartering. I swapped him a lathe, some fishing tackle, and a few other things I had, plus enough cash to do the deal. The guy was one of those people who always has a lot of unfinished projects going. He didn't have the coupe very long, and he wasn't intent on keeping it."

The old hot rod was exactly what Gerard wanted. But whose car had it been?

Christensen successfully played detective. He found a 1949 Pennsylvania registration in the coupe, and, after some effort, he traced it back to Bill Kelly of Warminster, Pennsylvania, who was still living in his old suburban Philadelphia neighborhood. Kelly was delighted to hear that his old hot rod had resurfaced. He was even happier when he learned that the coupe remained substantially the way it had been when he owned it.

Looking back, Bill Kelly was one lucky kid in 1948. His dad, the late Thomas Kelly, bought him a stock 1932 coupe for the princely sum of $200 when young

Bill was just 15, so his dad's name was on that early registration. "We used to walk to school in those days, really," Kelly told me, when I contacted him by phone. "I couldn't title the car until 1949 when I was sixteen."

Kelly thinks his coupe may have come from California, but it wasn't a hot rod when his dad bought it. "It was stock and it was in beat-up shape," he recalled. "We started to see cars from California in the magazines and we jumped right in. I had a lot of help from guys who were involved in stock car racing." Bill said his dad was into stock car racing, too, and he helped him channel the coupe.

"The engine was a flathead V-8 at first," Kelly continued. "We were sorta' sneaky," he said with a chuckle. "The stock car [Sportsman Class racing] guys helped with a lot of parts other people didn't have, like milled and modified cast-iron heads and really good ignition made from stock Ford parts. In fact," he noted proudly, "I had a better ignition system than the stuff you could order from California through the mail." The flathead's displacement was stock, Kelly recalled, "but it was virtually unbeatable. Hell, the car only weighed about two thousand pounds."

Kelly had many friends in the now 50-plus-year-old Modifiers car club of Philadelphia. "They wanted me to join," he said, "but I was an outlaw. I'd race anybody at the drop of a hat." When people did start beating him in impromptu races, in the early 1950s, Kelly replaced the flathead with a 303ci OHV V-8 from an Olds 88, and the fragile Ford tranny gave way to a burly LaSalle three-speed top loader. Kelly says his coupe was unbeatable with that Olds motor. "Motorcycles would see me," he laughs, "and they'd go the other way."

But he wanted even more speed.

"Then I got a buy on a Cadillac. I used to go over to New Jersey to race at night. Here was this engine—it was all in a box. It had a wild Isky cam, a Vertex magneto, and a C-T stroker kit. They had to notch the cylinder walls for clearance. And I got the whole thing for three hundred bucks! It was very fast with that engine."

Later, Bill's coupe ran hotter due to a blown Caddy. The car's basic appearance stayed the same, but more and more horsepower found its way into the engine compartment. Kelly said he never bothered with a hood. "It just added weight, you know."

"I drove it everywhere," he noted proudly. "If there was a race, I was there." You quickly understand, he means that he attended stock car and drag races as a spectator, but he also took on all comers on the street. Says Gerard Christensen, "Apparently, Kelly garnered quite a reputation as a hell-raiser while tooling his coupe in and around the streets of Philadelphia."

Were cops a problem, we wondered. "Yeah, I had to avoid 'em," said Kelly, hinting that he outran the law once or twice. "Sometimes it was pretty close."

"One night," he recalled, "I was cruising the boulevard [even today, Philadelphians all refer to Roosevelt Boulevard simply as 'the Boulevard'] when another '32 coupe pulls alongside me. I had small front tires and a straight front axle. He had a dropped front axle. Other than that, our cars were pretty similar. Turned out, he was the son of a family that owned a big funeral home. Of course, we both took off when the light changed. But mine was faster."

Kelly ran his car "mostly on the street," but he also competed at the Lancaster US 30 Drag-O-Way and at the York Drag-O-Way. Kelly claims his car would run in the 11s. Christensen actually found some of the old timing tickets in the car when he bought it. Kelly also had a brief stint driving his 1932 as a pace car at the Langhorne Speedway, but he says he quit because the coupe's low grille was bottoming out in the deep ruts on the track.

Kelly praised his old car's sturdy Cad/LaSalle three-speed. "It's still in there," but he acknowledges the 1940 Ford rear end was weak. "We used to twist 'em up like pretzels," he says, using a familiar reference in a city that's famous for them. Kelly told Christensen he even drove the car into Manhattan. On one wild ride, he claimed the passenger's suicide door flew open and kinked the body. Gerard says he's located a small dent in the upper rear quarter panel, exactly where the door handle would have hit.

Bill Kelly ran his coupe hard from 1948 to the late 1950s, and when he finally did sell it, the engine was gone. Why did he let it go? "After a while," Kelly said, a bit wistfully, "it was like a millstone around my neck. You know, we were always changing our cars in those days. Half the time, it was apart. I had the engine out; there was always something that hadda be done to it. I like cars, but you know . . . so I sold it."

The first guy who bought it just put it in a garage. "It had half a dozen owners after him, and the car was raced again," Kelly said, "but obviously, no one changed it substantially. They still kept that purple paint. At one point someone poked holes in the back and installed push bars." Kelly told Christensen that he never put on those Chevy lights or the writing on the deck lid. But very little else was different when it was found.

Over time, he lost touch with his old car, but Bill Kelly never did get hot rodding out of his sytem. A few years ago, he built a small-block V-8-engined Vega that, from the sound of things, might have given his old coupe a run for its money. And he admires today's hot rods. "They look good," he says, "and they should, considering what they cost."

You can tell Kelly's still practical. Success in his era of hot rodding depended on searching wrecking yards for usable parts. And like many older rodders, the guys who scrounged, salvaged, or hand-made most of their parts, he's amazed at what you can buy over the counter or through the mail. "But I don't know about that square roll bar stuff," he said. "That must have been New York."

He still has a great sense of humor. "A lot of hot rodders I see today have gray hair and [they're with] young babes. Their wives probably threw 'em out for messing with cars. The young ones don't know any better."

Bill Kelly "thinks it's great" that Christensen is preserving his car. But he's very modest about it. "I've told a lot of the guys," he says. "And they roared. There were a lot nicer cars than mine around. We had a guy with a chopped '39 coupe with an Olds in it, plenty of '40 Fords and some other '32s. There was a lot of stuff," he says, reflectively. "But mine is the only one that survived."

Gerard Christensen likes the fact that Bill Kelly's old coupe looks "substantially the way it did when I dug it out of the barn." But he confesses to one prejudice. "I've never liked the way cars looked when they're just channeled. They look out of proportion, a bit cartoony," he said.

So he took the old coupe back to Dave Simard's shop, East Coast Custom, in Leominster, Massachusetts, for some sympathetic metalwork. After the photos were taken, Gerard confesses: "I had Dave chop the top three and one-half inches. That's my one and only real change in its basic appearance. But we didn't fill the roof insert," he said, "and we kept as much of the old paint as we could. Dave saved and re-cut the old Ford script glass. We even preserved those decals on the window.

"The car now runs a '49 Cad 331 with a Weiand Drag Star manifold, six Stromberg 97 carbs, Spalding Flamethrower ignition, original Belond tube headers, and Offy valve covers," Christensen says. "It's still got the same shortened '37 Lasalle trans, banjo rear, and SW gages in the red metalflake dash insert that Bill Kelly installed way back when."

The sheetmetal floor was unusable, so Dave Simard built a new floor for the car and attached it to a second set of abbreviated 1932 rails. Says Simard, "I never did this before, but it seemed like the way to go in this case. Now the body is attached to the new sub-rails, which are really a second set of shortened deuce rails, bolted to the car's actual frame. This way, the body has some structural integrity, and if Gerard wants, he can take it right off the real frame. When you open the doors, it still looks like a 'regular' channeled '32."

By way of explanation, years ago, when cars were channeled, most guys simply cut or torched away the original floor, dropped the body the amount they wanted, and welded the whole thing together with a new floor and a few angle iron supports. It was often done rather crudely, so Simard's modification represents a better solution. When Christensen bought the coupe, it had a makeshift gas tank in the trunk. Simard's shop fabricated a new tank before they returned the car to Christensen.

Here's the car as it rolled out of a 40-year storage. Christensen has refurbished the car mechanically, but has decided to leave the cosmetics untouched. The authentic, original car has been displayed at the prestigious Saratoga Auto Museum in Saratoga Springs, New York. *Girard Christensen collection*

"You can see why so many cars were channeled on the East Coast." Gerard Christensen says. "A couple of guys could do it in a day the way they did it in the old days." After watching how difficult it was for Dave to chop this car, he has a renewed appreciation for that process. And he's quick to say he agonized over whether to change the coupe's "original" look.

"It tortured me to make that decision." he admits, "but I wouldn't have been happy if we hadn't done it. My dad was a powerboat racer and I didn't do much with hot rods when I was a kid. But I always imagined having a chopped and channeled '32 coupe."

And now he has one. Other than that top chop, Christensen vows, "I'm not changing anything. From now on, the only thing past 1960 in this coupe will be the gasoline."

The Swindler
in the Alley

When I was a preteen, no drag car captured my heart like the blue 1941 Willys coupe that was campaigned by the legendary team Stone, Woods & Cook. I don't know what it was about that car—it was not the newest or fastest drag car on the circuit—but it captured my imagination as the ultimate hot rod/drag racer. My friend Buzzy Brischler and I would stare at the coupe in magazines. Buzzy even built a Revell model of the car.

Apparently Buzzy and I weren't alone in our opinions; a poll was conducted on the National Hot Rod Association's website, and the same coupe that captured our young imaginations was voted overwhelmingly by enthusiasts as their favorite race car of all-time. That's quite a testament to a pre–World War II economy car.

The coupe was owned and built by Fred Stone and Tim Woods—both successful Los Angeles–area building contractors—and was driven by Doug "Cookie" Cook. The car was originally powered by a 425-cubic-inch, blown Oldsmobile, but later renditions were powered by blown Chrysler Hemis. But the car was truly greater than the sum of its parts.

First off, the car's aesthetics were flawless; the rake, fit, and finish were show quality. The Willys coupe featured a blue and white tucked and rolled interior that was stitched by legendary upholsterer Eddie Martinez. Ed "Big Daddy" Roth applied the tasteful pinstriping and lettering. And the car was the-best-of-the-best in the A- and B-Gas classes.

Most kids my age first became enamored with the Stone, Woods & Cook Willys by purchasing one of the three million model kits that Revell produced in 1963.

Besides breaking speed records on the track, eventually becoming the first gasser to break 150 miles per hour in 1964, the team was breaking other barriers: the team, owned by Fred Stone, Tim and Leonard Woods, and Doug Cook,was the first racially integrated professional drag racing team in history. Partner Tim Woods owned one of the largest minority-owned construction companies in the West.

The original Willys campaigned by the team, called *Swindler II* (because it replaced *Swindler I*, a 1941 Studebaker sedan) was but the first of several generations of the team's Willys gassers. Cars were replaced because of crash damage and updating. But it was *Swindler II* that put the team on the map, achieved national recognition, and became the car that Revell modeled for their popular kit.

Swindler II was retired from the track in 1966 after a racing accident, replaced by *Swindler A*. *Swindler II* was traded to Cal Automotive for a fiberglass Mustang body for a new Stone, Woods & Cook project called *The Dark Horse*. Cal Automotive painted their logo on the deck lid and chained it to a light post in their parking lot as a sign.

An engine builder named Paul Gammi would drive by the car every day and look at the historic racer from a past era just wasting away. At the time, Gammi was building a blown Chrysler Hemi for a guy who was going to reward his son, who

Even though the previous owner had sanded off the lettering, the unmistakable logo was still obvious. The car had been a fan favorite in the 1960s. Revell sold three million model kits of the car. *Joe Troilo*

was in Vietnam. When the engine was completed, the man said he needed a car, so Gammi said, "I know just the car," and purchased the coupe from Cal Automotive for $800. But before the project was completed, the father came in and informed Gammi that his son was just killed and that he should sell the car, engine, and all the parts.

Gammi sold the car to a man named Cotton Coltharp, who worked for Holman-Moody in Charlotte, North Carolina. Coltharp was a street rodder, so the car was brought east to North Carolina. In 1969, Coltharp sold the car through *Drag News* for $900 to Ron Ladley, who was known as the Willys Man. He had a reputation for restoring rather than modifying Willys cars. His plan was to restore the famous drag coupe as a street rod.

"As a kid, I drag raced my own small-block Chevy powered Willys coupe," said Joe Troilo of Avondale, Pennsylvania. "I never got to race against these guys [Stone, Woods & Cook], because mine was just a penny-pincher deal. But I did see these guys race on occasion and was always impressed."

The Willys became outdated for drag racing in 1968, with more modern body styles being preferred by racers. Because Willys coupes were being taken off the track, many of them were being converted to street use. Troilo began to convert his Chevy-powered coupe into a street rod, but he needed more parts.

Time, marriage, and a tour in Vietnam delayed Troilo's street rod conversion, but in 1972, when he came home, he opened the weekly *Philadelphia Bullittin* newspaper and saw an ad for a Willys body and parts for sale. The parts were about 30 miles from Avondale in Philadelphia.

Few people knew when Troilo pulled into hot rod meets that his super sanitary Willy rod was once a famous drag car. The car maintained the same Martinez tucked and rolled interior as when it actively raced, though. *Joe Troilo*

"When I got there, I was by myself and met Ron Ladley," said Troilo. "We walked down this little alley to his garage, which was behind his house. And when he opened the door, I almost fell on the floor, because it was the Stone, Woods & Cook car, still lettered with racing wheels, interior and headlights still in place.

"There was no engine or transmission. You can imagine the look on my face.

"Ron wanted one thousand dollars for the car. I had two hundred dollars with me, which I gave him. I asked him, 'Will this hold the car for a couple of hours?' He said yes, so I called my parents and told them there would be a guy stopping by the house with a rollback truck. They should give him eight hundred dollars and I'd explain later. I wasn't relieved until I got the car home."

Troilo converted the gasser into an attractive street rod, but admirers of the car had no way to tell the car was actually the most famous Willys coupe in existence. Fortunately all the original racing parts where hanging on his garage wall.

In 1978, when his family outgrew the small coupe with no back seat, Troilo sold the car to Mike Wales of New Jersey. Wales had several street rods, so he and Troilo became friends after seeing each other at various rod runs. Wales

The happy ending is when Troilo sold the Willys to Mike Wales in 1978, Wales contracted Troilo to restore the car to its original racing condition. *Joe Troilo*

kept reminding Troilo that he'd like to one day buy the car, so no advertising was necessary when it was time to sell.

Wales used the car as a street rod for a number of years, but intended to one day restore it back to the Stone, Woods & Cook gasser.

"Mike and I had an agreement that if he decided to sell the Willys, I would have the first option to buy it back," said Troilo. "I actually tried to buy it back for years—I was trying to take advantage of him—because he was transferred to Chicago and the car was still in New Jersey. He lost storage, but he never sold me the car."

In 2001, after 23 years of ownership, the conversion from street car back to race car began in earnest. Wales contracted Troilo to restore the car back to the way it looked in 1962. He reinstalled many of the original parts he had in his garage, down to reinstalling the dash-mounted tachometer into holes he had brazed up in 1972. The coupe still has the Martinez tucked and rolled interior that was installed in 1961.

Now that the Willys is restored, Wales hints to his next vintage car quest. "The team used to tow this coupe around the country behind a 1954 Ford two-door station wagon that was painted and lettered like the car," he said. "I've been looking out for one of those because I think it would be a neat beater to drive around in.

"The Ford wagon had an Oldsmobile engine in it, so if the race car launched an engine at the track, they would pull the engine out of the wagon and use it in the Willys. Then after the race, they would go to a junkyard and try to find a motor so they could get the tow car back down the road."

At the 2009 Hot Rod Reunion in Bakersfield, California, the featured team was Stone, Woods & Cook. *Swindler II* was proudly displayed by Mike Wales, who was accompanied by previous owner and restorer Joe Troilo. Thousands of enthusiasts stopped to inspect the car that many had become infatuated with as kids.

CHAPTER THREE

Hollywood Machines

The Green Hornet
Strikes Again

How many youths have fallen in love with a car that starred on their favorite television show or movie? I've met folks who have had lifelong passions for the Batmobile, the Monkeemobile, and the green Mustang fastback from the movie *Bullitt*.

Karl Kirchner can't explain why he fell in love with the *Black Beauty* from the *Green Hornet* television series.

"Even as a kid, I just really liked that particular car," said Kirchner, 46, from Spartanburg, South Carolina. "I was just a little kid, three or four years old, but I liked the show more than Batman, because it was more serious.

"I even had a Corgi toy of the car."

A lifelong quest ensued for Kirchner as he sought information on the innovative television show car.

I know a thing or two about the *Black Beauty* as well. The car was built by customizer Dean Jeffries, who said it is one of the favorite cars he has built in his long career. I wrote the book *Dean Jeffries: 50 Fabulous Years in Hot Rods, Racing & Film* (MBI Publishing Company, 2009), which chronicles this fascinating man's career.

The *Black Beauty* started life as a 1966 Chrysler Imperial and provided transport for the crime-fighting duo of the Green Hornet (played by Van Williams) and his faithful sidekick, Kato (played by Bruce Lee).

The Imperial was radically modified with crime-fighting equipment, including a front grille-mounted cannon and a pair of rocket launchers below each headlight. The rear of the car featured bumpers that flipped open to reveal rockets and flamethrowers. Behind the rear wheels were two small brushes that would sweep away tire tracks on dirt roads.

But even though the *Black Beauty* featured dozens of radical—albeit fictional—options, most viewers never truly connected with the car the way fans of the Batman series connected with the Batmobile.

"They messed it up," said Jeffries when I interviewed him for his biography. "They made me paint the car black and they only used it for night shots. You couldn't see it!"

So even though Jeffries invested blood, sweat, and tears building the two *Black Beauties*, the car went unappreciated among most viewers.

Except Karl Kirchner.

The show was cancelled after only one season, and the studio offered Jeffries the pair of cars for $1,500. When he turned down the offer, the cars fell into obscurity. The No. 1 car, which was used for most of the television production, was restored and eventually sold to the Petersen Automotive Museum in Los Angeles.

"The first car resurfaced in 1991, and everyone thought it was the only car that was built," said Kirchner. "It had been privately owned and Dean [Jeffries] restored the car for the owner."

This is how *Green Hornet* enthusiast Karl Kirchner discovered his dream car, the *Black Beauty*. The Dean Jeffries' design was crammed into a tight Michigan garage. Kirchner made friends with the elderly female owner. When she passed away, her heirs thought that he would be the ideal next owner. *Karl Kirchner*

But Kirchner knew a second *Black Beauty* existed. The second car was used occasionally for the television program, but mostly for promotional displays and car shows.

Kirchner called Dean sometime in the late 1980s and asked him if he knew where the second *Black Beauty* might be. He responded, "No, but if I did, I would have bought it already."

"He kept pretty good track of his cars over the years," Kirchner said. "It bothered him that he didn't know where the other car was."

The second car was sold originally to *Green Hornet* producer William Dozier, who kept it until 1969. Fellow customizer George Barris negotiated with Dozier to sell the car to Jack Button, a collector who intended to build an auto museum at Disneyland. But the museum project fizzled, and in 1971, *Black Beauty* No. 2 was sold to a Mr. J.J. Born, but only after the car was "modified" by George Barris with new paint, pinstriping, and new wheels. In 1984 the car was sold for $10,000 to Constantine Tatooles, a cardio surgeon.

Eventually, *Black Beauty* was sold at a Kruse auction in Auburn, Indiana, to a 78-year-old woman, Opal Wall.

"Wall was single and a certified car nut," said Kirchner. "She also owned a black 1955 Ford Thunderbird, which she bought new, and a black 1969 Lincoln Mark III. She loved black cars.

"She bought it at the auction because she liked its looks and thought it looked similar to a presidential car. She displayed the car for two years in the Gilmore Museum in Kalamazoo, Michigan, then put [it] into storage a couple of blocks from her home."

Kirchner (pictured) purchased the car in 2001 and began a thorough restoration. This is how the car appears today. Kirchner hopes to reunite the *Black Beauty* with original builder Dean Jeffries at the Amelia Island Concours. *Karl Kirchner*

Kirchner still hadn't located the car, but through a stroke of luck, was given a couple of clues by the then owner of *Black Beauty* No. 1.

"Louis Ringe found paperwork on car No. 2 in the glove box of car No. 1," said Kirchner. "When he found out I was interested in it, he gave me the VIN. This was probably in 1999.

"Within twenty-four hours, I found out that a woman, who turned out to be Opal Wall, owned the car."

Kirchner called Wall's home, but there was no answer. He learned that he had to call earlier in the day, when Opal was in the part of her house where she could hear the phone.

Eventually they developed a telephone friendship because they both loved to talk about cars.

"Have you ever thought about selling the *Black Beauty*?" Kirchner asked Wall.

"Yes, people need to see this car," she answered. "Why don't you come up here to see it?"

So at the next opportunity Kirchner drove from his South Carolina home to Southern Michigan to see the car of his boyhood dreams.

Wall was apparently eagerly awaiting his arrival; as soon as Kirchner pulled in the driveway, she bolted out the front door and jumped into his car. She explained that the car was stored at a nearby garage owned by a heating and air conditioning business. When they got to the garage, just a few blocks away, they met the grumpy garage owner.

"He never took his eyes off of me," Kirchner said. "I walked around and looked at the car as best I could, because it was sandwiched between old Chevys.

"I looked under the hood and could barely squeeze between the cars to check the car's VIN. And it only had eleven thousand miles on the odometer. Once I saw that, I knew it was Jeffries' car."

Wall said he could take pictures of the car, but the grumpy garage owner jumped in and said no. But Wall gave Kirchner a Polaroid photo of the car.

"We drove back to her house and sat around talking price," he said. "She was receptive. But I wanted to give her time to talk it over with her family. So I drove home thinking all the way about owning that car."

He waited a few days, then called Wall. No answer. He called over and over for more than a month until one day a man answered. The man turned out to be Wall's nephew, and he told Kirchner that his aunt had a stroke and had fallen. She was in the hospital.

Kirchner sent flowers to her, which she appreciated, but less than 30 days later, she died. This was in June 2000.

"I kept track of obituary notices online," he said. "I found out through the courts that Wall's niece had been appointed executor of the estate. I told her I had been speaking to her aunt about purchasing the car. She said she wanted to talk to the man who owned car No. 1, as well as to George Barris."

In June 2001, a purchase was negotiated for the same amount that Kirchner and Wall had discussed a couple of years earlier.

When the paperwork was signed, Kirchner had the car shipped to South Carolina.

"Once home, I looked at it for a couple of years," he said. "It was beginning to show its age," he said. "It had cracked paint and the leather seat top was torn where Barris had customized it by gluing flashlights to it.

"After a few years of just looking at it, I decided to dive in and do a complete restoration. My first intention was to completely strip the car and rebuild it like Jeffries did, but then I realized if I did that, it would erase the fingerprints of Dean Jeffries."

A partial restoration complicated Kirchner's task, because instead of just purchasing and installing a hot rod wiring kit, he repaired the old, complicated wiring harness that Jeffries had constructed decades earlier. Most of the electric motors that actuated various special effects on the car were military-issued, so Kirchner had a difficult time sourcing replacement units.

"I've done probably a dozen restorations in my life, and by far, this is the most difficult and expensive car I've done," said Kirchner. "First of all, it's an

Imperial, and most of them probably wound up in demolition derbies. It's not a 'Cuda or a Road Runner, so people don't save parts, so finding them was a challenge.

"It has taken three to four years to restore the car, which is interesting, because Dean built the original car in just two to three weeks."

A Gullwing for
Big Dog Garage

Some of us have to search for old cars the old-fashioned way; opening our eyes as wide as possible as we drive down the street or keeping our ears open to hear rumors for old cars. Others of us have a real advantage and can request old car information on our own national television show.

Such is the luck of Jay Leno, host of the *Tonight Show with Jay Leno* on NBC.

If you read *The Vincent in the Barn* (Motorbooks, 2009), you may remember that Leno lucked into a rare Vincent Black Shadow barn find when he just happened to mention to viewers that he needed a Vincent gas tank that he dented over the weekend. The next day a gentleman called from Florida telling him that he didn't have a gas tank, but he did have a complete Black Shadow that he bought new when he was in the service decades earlier.

Leno has become America's best-known car collector, and he constantly gets phone calls and letters at his studio that the rest of us could only dream about.

This was the case recently when a letter arrived from a viewer saying that he had a vintage Arial motorcycle for sale. "This guy sends Jay a two-page letter talking about the bike," said Bernard Juchli, general manager of Leno's Big Dog Garage in Burbank. "Then on the bottom of the letter it says he also has a 1955 Mercedes 300SL for sale.

"So I asked Jay, 'Would you like to buy an Arial motorcycle?' and he said 'No, not really.' Then I asked him if he had any interest in a Mercedes Gullwing, and that piqued his interest."

The Mercedes-Benz 300SL Gullwing is one of the most iconic sports cars of all-time. It was made famous by the operation of its doors, which opened up instead of out; the car resembled a seagull with its wings outstretched. Gullwings are powered by a powerful straight six-cylinder engine, a toned-down version of the engine that enabled the legendary Sir Sterling Moss to win the 1,000-mile 1955 Mille Miglia through the Italian Alps in a time so fast that it has never been beaten.

Leno has always had a hankering to own a Gullwing. Before his comedy career took off, he worked as a mechanic on old Mercedes-Benz models in the Boston area.

"The car was out in Orange County somewhere, and apparently had been stored in a shipping container behind the guy's business since 1983," said Juchli.

Entertainer Jay Leno purchased this iconic Mercedes 300SL Gullwing after it had sat in a storage container for 35 years. The Gullwing was raced throughout California on road courses such as Riverside. The car's interior had been stitched by noted upholsterer Tony Nancy. *Tom Cotter*

Juchli is the man responsible for managing Leno's huge collection, which consists of about 130 cars and 70 motorcycles. "I had a Jaguar shop up in the San Francisco Bay Area, and Jay sent his XK120 engine for me to modify to racing specs," he said. "Eventually Jay realized it would be cheaper for him to hire me to manage his collection than to send projects to my shop.

"I was hired to set up the shop so we could actually do work and perform our own restorations instead of sending them out to other shops. But Jay likes to be involved in the process, and he gets his hands dirty all the time."

Big Dog Garage's staff of seven now performs complete restorations and has fabricated a number of cars from the ground up.

"The engine was out of the Gullwing when I bought the car," said Leno. "It was all in pieces. This is how I found it. So far we've done the brakes and the gauges over.

"My plan is to drive it like this; keep it a beater Gullwing."

Leno said the car was put into a storage container at least 35 years ago.

"It just sat," he said. "It was one of those things where the owner intended to restore it, but he never quite got around to it."

Leno said he hears about many cars because he has a reputation for paying the asking amount for cars and people know he's not going to resell them for a profit.

"And when you deal with older guys, especially guys with no kids, they want to know that their stuff is going to a good home," he said. "They'll say, 'If you promise to take care of it, I'll sell it for this much.'"

As a longtime admirer of the Gullwing sports car, Leno is clearly pleased with his new purchase. "The nice thing about this car is that even though it was a race car, it's never been hit," he said. "Look how nicely the doors close.

"This car was raced at Riverside. I have pictures of it running there.

"It has just seventy-three thousand miles, and I'm just the third owner."

He went on to say that the car has no rust, but unfortunately he was missing the factory belly pans.

"I believe the car was

The Candy Apple paint, which had been applied decades earlier by the legendary Junior Conway, had seen better days. But Leno plans to keep the body as-is and will only refurbish the mechanicals. *Tom Cotter*

originally silver, but sometime in the 1960s or early 1970s, it became sort of a hot rod. It was painted by Junior Conway of Junior's House of Colors in a candy apple red. And Tony Nancy, another famous hot rod guy from the 1960s, stitched the interior.

"It was just an old sports car back then."

The Producer's Imperial

Jay Leno admits there is nothing special about a 1967 Chrysler Imperial LaBaron, and it's certainly not a car he ever dreamed about owning. But this particular car was different enough that he decided to take a look, and he's glad that he did.

"I got a call from an old boy at my office," said Leno. "He said 'My name is Leo, I'm ninety-three years old, and I can't drive anymore. I want you to buy my car.'"

Leno asked what type of car he had for sale, hoping it would be a rare Duesenberg or Bugatti. But when Leo said that he owned a 1967 Chrysler Imperial LaBaron, Leno was eager to end the phone conversation as quickly as possible.

"I told him I wasn't really looking for one of those, but Leo said, 'Oh, no, no, you'll like this one,'" said Leno. "He told me it was a two-door with dual air conditioning."

"They only made eighteen of those in 1967," said Leo. "I bought it new and had it serviced at my home twice a month by a Chrysler mechanic."

Reluctantly, Leno agreed to take a look at the car.

"Where do you live?" Leno asked.

"I live on Sunset Boulevard in Beverly Hills," said Leo.

"Oh, what do you do for a living?" asked Leno.

"I'm an old-time movie producer," said Leo, as he rattled off a few movie titles to Leno.

Armed with Leo's address, Leno went up and down Sunset Boulevard looking for Leo's address. "I felt like William Holden in the movie *Sunset Boulevard*."

Finally he sees Leo's house number, adjacent to a long driveway going off the street. He turns into the driveway and proceeds up to the house.

"It was a 1940s Beverly Hills mansion," said Leno. "So I pull in front of his house, and he's standing in the driveway with a smoking jacket and an ascot. Standing next to Leo is another gray-haired guy around seventy years old."

"Jay, this is my mechanic from Chrysler, and he wants to retire, so I have to get rid of the car," said Leo.

So the three men walked inside the garage to look at the Chrysler. Leno said that it was like a brand-new 1967 Chrysler Imperial.

Leo explained the purchase of the car. "When I bought this thing, I was so afraid I was going to have an accident," he said. "So I bought two of everything."

Comedian and car collector extraordinaire Jay Leno couldn't say no to Leo. Leo purchased the Imperial new in 1967, along with almost every spare part available for the car. The car had been serviced twice a month by a Chrysler mechanic since new, but at 93 years of age, Leo could no longer drive. *Tom Cotter*

Leo opened up the other side of the garage, revealing brand-new parts still wrapped in paper.

"He had new bumpers, grilles, headlights, windshield wiper motors, electric window motors—basically everything you would need to replace if you bought a car for life," said Leno.

"If you buy the car, all this crap goes with it," said Leo.

Leno took a look around the car.

"Now I have to buy it," he says he thought to himself. "I can't not buy it. I mean, look at it; it's a brand-new '67 Chrysler.

"When we got it back to the shop, it was smoking a little bit. So we pulled the engine and did a clean-up on it."

Leno said the most impressive thing about the car is that everything works so well.

"It has electric everything," said Leno. "It has the thin A-pillar with the panoramic windshield. But this car has the exact opposite of road feel; you drive with one finger, you lightly touch the brake. It's incredibly smooth.

"This car represents the last days of old technology. It's one of the very last big cars where the huge engine, big carburetor, and three-speed Torqueflite transmission had all been perfected. Gas mileage is abysmal, though."

Leno says the car's redeeming grace is when it is driven at 70 miles per hour down the freeway.

"The dual air conditioners have you freezing in less than a minute when you throw the switch on," he said. "The car has two a/c compressors with units in the front and rear passenger compartments.

"The only feature this car doesn't have is a portable office, which believe it or not had a desk and a swivel passenger seat."

The car is quite impressive. The size and condition of the Chrysler make it appear new. Leno said the paint had been touched up, but the vinyl top is still original.

"I think Leo had driven the car up until they took his driver's license at ninety-three years old," said Leno. "He just wanted it to go to a good home. It's wonderful to drive. I use it a lot, especially in the summertime."

Leno said that one reason so few of these models exist is because many of them were used in demolition derbies because of their tank-like construction.

"This is obviously a case of buying the story and getting the car thrown in on the deal," he said.

CHAPTER FOUR

International
Intrigue

The Price of War

Young people often travel to "find themselves." It's a rite of passage for many to travel to the end of the road; but most of the time that road ends in North America.

Midwesterner Bill Baker's road ended on the other side of the globe.

Baker grew up in Indianapolis, and cars were in his blood. His parents took an MG-TC on their honeymoon to the East Coast in 1948. His father campaigned Porsches in the 1950s at Sports Car Club of America races while his mother drove the same car in gymkhanas.

"I got a taste for cars from my parents, plus my grandfather used to restore Pierce Arrows after he retired as president of Firestone Steel," said Baker, 60.

Before he went to find himself, Baker owned a number of interesting cars, including the Olds 442 that his father bought new for him in 1967. His first sports car was a Mercedes-Benz 300SL Gullwing coupe. "I bought it from an ad in *Road & Track* and restored it myself," he said. He also purchased a Maserati 200si from an *AutoWeek* ad, a second Gullwing, a Jaguar XK140, and a Ferrari 356 GT4.

So when Baker took what Australians call a "walkabout," he didn't wind up on a sunny beach in Malibu or Key West. He went to Kuwait. As in the Persian Gulf. He knew, though, that no matter where he traveled, somehow cars would be involved.

"I had just gotten divorced, and I wanted to get away," he said. "While I was an engineering student at Purdue, my two best friends were from Kuwait. I heard about a highway project over there, so I applied."

Baker was hired for the job, so he put his Mercedes Gullwing into storage in a local farmer's barn.

"I didn't return soon, so eventually that farmer sold it," said Baker. "It is ironic, but my car probably became someone else's barn find!"

His new life in Kuwait consisted of a lot of work; 12-hour days, six days a week minimum. Initially he worked too much to pursue his automotive passions. But he did pay attention to the cars he saw driven on the Kuwait roads.

"There are so many cars in Kuwait," said Baker. "The Arabs are car-crazy."

Many of us have heard of the extravagant automotive habits of the very rich in that region. Baker confirms that many of those tales are true.

"I've seen guys get rid of cars just because they're tired of the color," he said. "They'll sell it off for a pittance of what they're worth, or they just stick them in the corner of their garage.

"I've been in guys' garages that would blow your mind. I saw one Shelby GT500, and when I opened the hood, it had a four-cam Indy car engine. The wealthy sheik that owned the car told me he ordered it from Shelby with this engine."

Baker tells of original-family-owned Ferraris he has seen that will never be sold. "Even though the sons of the deceased sheik have no interest in it, they'll never get rid of it because their father bought it new.

"In many ways, it's still like the Middle Ages over there, where kings are kings, and it's hard for anyone else to break in."

Eventually Baker began to pursue some of the exotic cars that he discovered. He explains that many of those cars—F-40 and F-50 Ferraris, Porsche Turbos, etc.—were given to young Arabs for Eid, a religious festival when sons of wealthy men turn 16 years old. Many of those cars eventually would be totaled, as their young and inexperienced owners crashed them at high speeds into stationary objects, or they were put into long-term storage in the family garage.

One car Baker is most proud of owning was the 1975 Porsche 911 Carrera Targa (VIN 911-561.0151) he purchased in 1989. According to Baker, the car was especially built for a wealthy Arab and was the only one like it in the world.

As confirmed by documentation from the Porsche factory, the car is the only 1975 Porsche that was built with Turbo-look bodywork.

"It was originally ordered by an Iranian heritage family that walked into the Porsche dealership and ordered a very special, one-of-a-kind car," said Baker. "And they got it. They certainly had their own idea as far as color is concerned. It had raspberry exterior paint with white leather interior and red copper carpeting. Not for everyone, but different."

The Porsche was ordered fully optioned, including gold alloy wheels, gold Carrera stripes, chrome trim, sport steering wheel, and short wave radio adaptor. Mr. Mohammed Reza Yousuf Behbehani, the car's original owner, paid more than DM 55,000 for the car in 1975—certainly a princely sum for the day.

Baker was proud of his new discovery. It was certainly a special car that he intended to own for a long time. Less than a year later, though, he lost it.

Do you remember what happened in Kuwait in 1990? That was when President George H.W. Bush sent American troops to the Persian Gulf to defeat Saddam Hussein's army.

"I was in Switzerland at the time inquiring about enrolling in an international MBA," said Baker. "But while I was gone, the Iraqi Army invaded Kuwait. I never saw my car again."

While Baker was sitting in Switzerland waiting for the war to end, the Iraqi Army helped themselves to Baker's Porsche, as well as his Mercedes-Benz G-Wagon, a Honda café-racer motorcycle, and his Beneteau 38-foot racing boat.

"They also went through all my clothes and all my good stuff," he said.

"But at least I didn't lose my life. Luckily I was out of the country, but many of my friends were tortured and the sister of a friend was tortured for a month and then killed."

When Baker returned to his Persian Gulf home, he had a tough time sorting through his possessions. He also found out the cruel fact that because he didn't have the "war coverage" option on his insurance policy, it was impossible for him to be reimbursed for his losses.

"I moved back in March 1991, a month after Liberation," he said. "I walked along the Highway to Hell, where burned tanks littered the six-lane highway.

"I just tried to go on with life like before, which was tough."

In an effort to retrieve his Porsche, Baker filed a stolen properties report with the Kuwait police. The police required documentation on the car, so they knew what they were looking for. He contacted Porsche in Germany in an effort to obtain official documents on the car's build. That's where he hit a brick wall.

Initially the Porsche factory denied that the Turbo bodywork was installed at the factory. "No Turbo-look body was made for the 1975 911 Targa," was the response he received from Stuttgart. "Sorry we can't solve this mystery."

But Baker was unrelenting in his effort to convince the factory that he indeed owned such a car. He just felt that nobody at the factory cared to look into the matter.

Finally, he received a letter from Porsche clearing up the matter. "Upon receipt of your fax, we—Technical Service—started a major investigation as to how exactly and most importantly, why your Porsche was built with the options as can be seen from the photos you sent us. With the help of our production facilities and our extensive research, we were able to find specific information concerning your very special and one of a kind 1975 Carrera Targa Turbo-look."

Another letter stated: "Our records show further that the Turbo-look modifications were indeed performed during the production of the vehicle. Since the actual Turbo-look option was first offered at a much later date, your Porsche can be considered as one of the first vehicles to be built with the special option. We presume that this is the only 1975 Carrera Targa Turbo-look that was ever manufactured in 1975. We wish you many pleasant driving miles with your unique Porsche." The letter was signed by G. Nonnenmacher and O. Lang.

Unfortunately the Porsche factory never returned the photos he sent them, and because his home was ravaged, all his cameras, prints, and negatives were ruined. So there are no photos to illustrate this intriguing story.

In 1995, Baker moved to Dubai and married a woman from Russia. And in a second attempt to find himself, he bought a Harley-Davidson Softtail. He brags about the aggressive rides he has taken. "I rode that Harley solo from

Kuwait to Dubai nonstop," he said. "That's one thousand three hundred fifty kilometers in twelve hours.

"But for the time being, I'm out of the car hobby. When you're as transient as I am, I shouldn't get into cars again."

So whatever became of the princely, one-of-a-kind Porsche?

Baker attempted to find out, but never did. But like so many other exotic cars lost during that brief war, he has an idea.

"I believe they gave my car to Saddam's son, Uday," said Baker. "He was a car nut, but he was also crazy.

"He killed one of his father's favorite bodyguards, so I believe Saddam had the car burned along with many of Uday's other cars in his collection. Either that or the car is still in Iraq hidden somewhere."

Baker has come to terms, however, with the fact that he'll never see that car again.

San Juan's Secrets

Jaime del Valle has the car bug real bad. It started out when he was a kid, and it got so bad, he was almost living in the street. He was into MGAs in a big way.

"My mother wanted to throw me out of the house," said del Valle, 54, who owns the only Jaguar dealership in Puerto Rico. "I had twenty-seven MGAs around her house.

"Of course back then, it was the only way to get parts for your car. You could buy a whole MGA back then for just three hundred dollars."

The MGA obsession led to other automotive obsessions. Today, almost 40 years after the episode with his mother, del Valle owns Jaguar Puerto Rico and somewhere between 35 and 40 collector cars.

"My wife says I own too many, but I say I still need plenty," he said.

"I'm a very happy Jaguar dealer these days," he said. "It's because the quality of the cars are so good now. But that means my shop is dead, because the cars are not breaking down anymore."

Despite his knowledge and obsession, a terrific collector car sat under his nose for many years.

What could be better than a free MG, especially when your lawyer asks you to take it away? This 1934 MG PA was photographed soon after it became an occupant in Jamie del Valle's cluttered MG garage. *Jamie del Valle*

Del Valle's attorney, Elena Gonzales, has represented him and his dealership for at least 14 years. She continually told her client about a "small foreign car" that her father had left in her garage. "Small foreign car" didn't sound like something del Valle wanted in his collection. Was it a Volkswagen Beetle, a rusty Datsun B210, or a Fiat sedan?

Wouldn't you know it . . . it was an MG.

"Fourteen years she's asked me to come and take this car, and I ignored her," said del Valle. "She never told me what it was.

"Finally she called me last year and told me she was doing a Christmas clean-up. She said, 'If you don't pick up the car, I'm going to throw it away.'"

When del Valle walked into Gonzales' garage, he was blown away; it was a complete 1934 MG PA. It would be a nice addition to the MG TC, MG TD, and MG A that were already sitting in his garage.

"I contacted the London MG Club in England, and they said the car had definitely been lost since 1934, and then it pops up in Puerto Rico" he said. "They told me the car was originally built in black with oxblood interior. That's a beautiful combination, and I'm having the car restored to those colors now."

Del Valle said the early MG has some unusual features. "Mounted on the four-cylinder engine is a combination generator and oil pump in one unit," he said. "I've never seen anything like that."

He said the only items that have been modified are the brakes. "My lawyer's son started to convert the car to Datsun disc brakes," said del Valle. "Thankfully, whoever was 'fixing up' that car never completed the job."

The Truth Behind
the Barn-Find Hoax
of the Century

By Wolfgang Blaube

O ne of the infamous barn-find tales is about an exotic car for sale for
$1,000—because a dead body had been lying in it for three weeks.
Sometimes the car is a Rolls-Royce Phantom, sometimes a Porsche 911 Turbo,
but the story is always the same. That story has been told for decades, and it's
nothing more than an urban legend.

If you like those fairy tales about great cars, here's an even more fantastic
automotive tale:

*"A New York man retired. He wanted to use his retirement money wisely, so
it would last, and decided to buy a home and a few acres in Portugal. The modest
farmhouse had been vacant for 15 years; the owner and wife both had died, and there
were no heirs. The house was sold to pay taxes. There had been several lookers, but the
large barn had steel doors, and they had been welded shut. Nobody wanted to go to
the extra expense to see what was in the barn, and it wasn't complimentary to the
property anyway . . . so, nobody made an offer on the place.*

*The New Yorker bought it at just over half of the property's worth; moved in, and
set about to tear in to the barn—curiosity was killing him. So, he and his wife bought
a generator and a couple of grinders and cut thru the welds. What was in the barn?"*

Does this story ring a bell? Of course. Hundreds of thousands—maybe even
millions—of car enthusiasts know this as one of the most circulated barn-find
stories in recent history. It circulated through countless Internet forums and
arrived in myriad email boxes all around the world.

The story's first page showed what the New York retiree discovered in
the barn after his grinder attack: a mind-blowing number of classic cars,
from a Lancia Flaminia Sport Zagato to several late-1950s Mercedes 300
Adenauers. Other pages displayed a fascinating gallery of the dust-covered
sleeping beauties:

"Amazing! Total value of all vehicles over 35 million! The man and his wife
had full title to the complete lot of vehicles. They're having a great retirement!"

Once the images disappear from the screen, the stunned viewer is left with
gaping mouth. Impressive. Impossible?

First of all: The barn is real. After an extensive search, I discovered it as well
as the real story behind the greatest barn find in history. But before I tell you the

truth, and nothing but the truth, let me recap the legend that spread around the worldwide web like an epidemic beginning in early 2007.

And they lived happily ever after . . . hello, anybody out there? Who believes in such a fairy tale? Obvious for the vast majority of us—the photos of the inside of the barn are sloppy—they are as authentic as the cars they portray. Discussions about the story began instantly; hundreds of web forums received more or less intelligent postings in detail.

One posts his opinion about "particulate matter contamination" of the vehicles. Another's philosophy talks about the long-term effect of pigeon dung on the automobile paint. Several speculate about the market values of the sleeping beauties, never mind that several models were badly misidentified: an old Formula Ford becomes a famous Grand Prix champion that was considered lost; an Abarth 1300 Scorpione becomes a Maserati Ghibli; a clearly recognizable Datsun 240Z becomes a Jaguar E-Type, then a Ferrari 250 GTO.

One conspiracy theorist predicts: "As everybody can see, all the cars have Dutch number plates, so they were obviously stolen and concealed, near Amsterdam." Another said the barn is a secret hiding place of a mystical Portuguese classic car mafia! Sensational criminal discoveries, either way.

In the United States, one forum includes skeptics who find fault with the fairy tale of the generator that allegedly powered the grinders; they believe that in a "threshold" country like Portugal, certainly no electric power generators exist, and actually welding the steel doors was absolutely impossible in light of those power deficiencies.

Some sly classic car freeloaders shoot from the hip: one pretends to know the New Yorker personally, and another offers to divulge his name for just EUR 1,000; another desperado claims to have the GPS coordinates of the barn ("deep in the woods and impossible to find")—choosing eBay.com as the sales channel for this exclusive knowledge; and finally one funster pipes up as an intimate friend of the barn buyer, offering the package of all 98 cars for just $5 million. Ninety-eight cars? Other sources report different quantities, varying from 26 to more than 200.

Eventually the worldwide classic car world decides that 180 vehicles exist. "Portugal Barn" becomes a hot topic of conversation among car enthusiasts around the globe, and Youtube's photo show—accompanied by an unbearable rant of "We are the Champions"—gathers enormous click-throughs. In March 2007, the global hype around the biggest barn find ever reaches a fever pitch.

During this time I spoke with my American colleague Tom Cotter. "Huge collections of cars don't just happen," he said. "They must have been accumulated on purpose by a specific person." This person has to be found, we both agree. And we decide on a collaboration.

The roughly 39,000-square-foot warehouse full of barn-find cars is in Portugal. *Wolfgang Blaube*

Soon after, Tom publishes a short article in *Sports Car Market*. He wrote that the owner is not a New York senior after all, but a Portuguese collector—who doesn't want himself or the exact location of his treasure identified. Incidentally, none of the 180 cars are for sale. Is this the end of the fairy tale? Or rather the beginning of a story about the collection's genesis?

After extensive research, a chance for the latter appears on the horizon. Hard-bitten proceedings with the collector follow, but eventually I am welcome to visit him in Portugal—without my camera. My negotiations continue, though, and months later, in early 2009, I finally receive a permit to produce the complete works including pictures.

After landing at the Lisbon airport, I follow the picturesque Tejo River upstream. After one and a half hours, I drive into a little village and wait. An S-Class Mercedes appears, and with a wave of finger its driver beckons me to follow. We end up on an old farm. There the S-Class driver introduces himself as Lourenço Ferreira de Almeida, dealer and renter of classic cars and the 26-year-old son of the collector. In reality the barn looks exactly as in the Internet photos—but significantly bigger. "Somewhere around thrity-nine thousand square-feet," Lourenço estimates, as he unlocks the heavy steel door.

Looking back, I remember the following two hours dimly. Here, a, a . . . no, there in the back, a . . . oh my God . . . at first this one . . . or better the one over there . . . hold on, this is a dream . . . isn't that, over there, a . . . unbelievable . . . .While Lourenço insightfully nods I meander through the endless rows of cars, feeling as if in a delirium. No, this is not the barn that I expected. This is the ultimate cathedral for classic car enthusiasts.

Finally I unpack my camera. There is no light or electricity in the barn; my flashlight batteries have to suffice. But the reduced number of cars makes my work easier. Since the photos appeared on the Internet two years ago, 103 cars have either been moved to another warehouse or sold; 189 cars remain; 292 total cars existed when the Internet photos came to light, not 180.

"Everyday classics," such as the Morris Minor, VW Beetle, or Citroën 2CV, were prevalent. But others, such as three Facel-Vega HK 500s (of about 250 surviving), three Mercedes-Benz 300 Adenauers, and a Citroën SM, were truly spectacular. Other classics included an Alfa Romeo Montreal and a 2600 Sprint Zagato, a Panhard PL 17 Tigre, a Kaiser Custom, and a Lotus 69 Formula 2. Exceptionally exotic cars included a 1956 Bristol 405 Saloon (1 out of 265 built) and a ravishing 1952 Simca 9 Sport with Facel body.

At eight o'clock in the evening Lourenço drags me—against my heavy resistance and with totally soiled clothing—out of the barn. But I am invited back the next day to take detail shots. And he promises a meeting with his father, António Ferreira de Almeida, owner of the huge collection.

António is a very decent, friendly man. He reflects back to the Portuguese Revolution of the Carnations, which occurred in the mid-1970s. "Back then dictatorship ended in our country and socialism seemed to be our next form of government," said Antonio, 60. "Everybody who owned a precious car stashed it in Spain or sold it for very, very little money." There appeared to be just one person interested in those older vehicles: a young, relatively wealthy used car dealer from Lisbon named António Ferreira de Almeida, the very man I was speaking with.

In his "labor of love" for old cars, he snatched up every car he could afford, not showing favoritism to manufacturer, country of origin, year, or condition. By the end of the 1970s, and still not 30 years old, António had accumulated some 100 cars. Within 10 years, the number had jumped to more than 300 cars. When his buying binge began to ebb in 1996, António owned almost 400 old vehicles, 25 percent of which were in good to excellent condition.

To store the other 75 percent, António rented an empty harvest depot up north of Lisbon in 1992 that had formerly been used by orange planters. Fifteen years later, this would become the legendary "Portuguese Barn." The barn consists of two wings, one huge room of 2,150 square yards, and four smaller, windowless side rooms about the same size. With help of his shabby Bedford-brand wrecker truck, it took António nearly six months to tow all the 292 cars—one by one—to their new home. When the barn was full, António locked the doors and left.

In 1999 he returned with a generator and a MIG welder. "Just prior to that time a sinister crowd moved into the neighborhood and the rate of burglaries increased," said António. "So I welded all the gates shut except of the small side door."

During one of his regular inspections in January 8, 2007, classic car dealer Manuel Menezes Morais accompanied him. Inside the barn Morais pulled out his pocket camera and shot 64 photos. A day later, at 10:00 a.m., he posted those photos on the "Curiosidades" section of his business' website, www.interclassico.com, and titled it with the rumor-spreading headline, "Ali Baba's Classic Car Cave." But he made no comment beyond that.

Not four hours later, the president of the classic car section of the National Automobile Club (ACP) nervously called António: his phone was ringing nonstop, and mass hysteria was imminent if Morais did not remove the photos from his web page immediately. He did so, but it was too late; someone had already copied the pictures and PowerPoint file and composed the fairy tale of the lucky New York buyer. And almost immediately the fable traveled on the global data highway at record speed.

Believe it or not, António is thrilled that the story went worldwide, but he keeps his gigantic collection in perspective. Yes, by now he would like to get rid

The roughly 39,000-square-foot warehouse full of barn-find cars is in Portugal. *Wolfgang Blaube*

of the most of the cars. He plans to keep just 100 historical vehicles in good condition. The majority of his favorites are spread throughout several underground parking garages throughout Lisbon and include the following: a Lancia Aurelia B24 Spider; Porsche 356 Carrera; Deutsch-Bonnet Le Mans; two more Adenauer Benzes; BMW 327/28 and two BMW 503s; two very early Citroën DS Chapron convertibles; Dino 246 GT; four out of his eleven Alfa 1900s in nine different body shapes; and ninety others. These are definitely-not-for-sale cars. But he did let me see and photograph this private stash.

Basically, all vehicles in the legendary barn are for sale, along with most of the ones António moved in 2007 to the other warehouse in Lisbon. Those were my photo session on the third day of my trip. Among many other cars, this collection included four of his six Lancia Aurelia B20 GTs, a Flaminia Zagato (that was identified as an Aston Martin in the Internet saga), and one extremely rare Abarth 1600 with Allemano bodywork.

In the face of this publicity, it will be disappointing to most enthusiasts to learn that most of the cars that were for sale were no real bargains. Ferreira de Almeida Sr. and Jr., are both familiar with market values, but even though none of the cars are dirt cheap, several are favorably priced.

Now Mr. Barn-find Tom Cotter and I almost feel sorry for having trampled down the myth of the "Portugal Barn." If it is any consolation for you, there are many other nice car-related urban legends: the immortal $1,000 Testarossa for example; or the story of the Arizona mechanic who attached a solid fuel rocket to the roof of his 1967 Chevy Impala and, according to the legend, traveled at a speed of 350 miles per hour before becoming airborne and after a 1.5-mile flight, ended up on a rock face with not much left besides a "How's My Driving?" bumper sticker.

However, the tale of the young Portuguese man who once bought nearly 400 cars is no less fantastic. At least it sounds way more probable than the story of the New York retiree. Sometimes real life just tells the best stories.

Wolfgang Blaube is a German journalist who writes about old cars for *Oldtimer Markt* (Germany; biggest classic car magazine worldwide after *Hemming's*), *Thoroughbred & Classic Cars* (Great Britain), *Classic & Sports Car* (Great Britain), *Excellence* (United States), and *La Vie d'Auto* (France; weekly classic car magazine and market leader in France).

The Fate of the
Sleeping Beauties

by Kay Hottendorff

If you mention "Sleeping Beauties" to serious car enthusiasts, they often know exactly what you are talking about: not the children's fairy tale, but the world-famous 1983 photo series that showed an extraordinary collection of classic automobiles seemingly rusting away in a French barn and garden, neglected by their owner. Cars of famous brands like Bugatti, Lancia, Ferrari, Alfa Romeo, Cord, and Aston Martin laying under thick layers of dust, spending their final days falling apart and abandoned.

These photos have been published many times (for example, in Automobile Quarterly *22/2 and 25/2 and in* The Cobra in the Barn*). The true story behind the collection and the fate of the more than 50 cars has never been told.*

Since the cars' existence was first made public in 1984, many have tried to find out what happened to the cars. Were they destroyed? Sold? Rusted into the ground? All leads quickly fizzled out, until three men determined to find the answer joined forces: Kay Hottendorff (41), an electrical engineer from Germany, and Ard op de Weegh (58), a school principal, and his son Arnoud op de Weegh (22), a student, both from the Netherlands.

Here Kay tells us about the amazing treasure hunt that spanned several years:

My passion for the Sleeping Beauties goes back to 1997, when I received a giant poster from my fiancée. The poster showed a dust-covered and decaying Bugatti amongst other 1930s classics. I have been addicted to classic cars since I was a young boy, but this photo intrigued me more than any I had ever seen. Since first seeing that image, the Sleeping Beauties haunted me.

Where? When? Who? Why? I had so many questions. Over the next nine years I gathered every bit of information available about the collection. The collection is shown in *Sleeping Beauties*, a book by Halwart Schrader and Herbert W. Hesselmann that was first published in 1986. The book contains a photo series and a fairy tale story about the collectioní's mysterious owner, "Pierre," his farm south of Paris, and his headstrong way of life. The story in the book ended in 1983.

During years of research, I found out the name of the Sleeping Beauties' owner and the location of his dust-covered antique car collection. "Pierre" turned out to be Michel Dovaz, one of the best-known wine critics in France and a legend in this field. Dovaz's cars had been removed from their original

One of most significant barn finds of the last 50 years was quietly stored behind these walls in the south of France. The famous Sleeping Beauties collection stirred imaginations around the world after it appeared in *Automobile Quarterly 22/2. Kay Hottendorff/Ard & Arnoud op de Weegh collection*

location south of Paris soon after the famous photo session. Some sources said all the cars had been sold. The sale theory was dubious due to the fact that very few of the cars were known to have been restored. A true story about the cars said that a museum containing 26 of the cars had been established temporarily in France around 1990.

The astonishing barn-find museum, where the cars had been displayed in unrestored condition and featured in various imaginative dioramas, included two 1930s Bugattis; a 1950s Aston Martin and Alfa Romeo; and a hobo mannequin appearing to reside in a 1960s Rolls-Royce.

But that information still did not satisfy me. What was the real story? Where had all those wonderful cars gone? I searched for individual cars on various Internet forums, hoping to find reliable clues regarding the current whereabouts of some of the Sleeping Beauties.

Toward the latter part of 2006, my questions on a car-related website forum attracted the attention of a young man some 230 miles southwest of me in the Netherlands. Arnoud op de Weegh, along with his father, Ard, had been researching the Sleeping Beauties collection since the end of 2002. Ard became interested in the collection after hearing about it from a colleague and fellow

Probably the most famous car in the Sleeping Beauties photo collection is this Bugatti Type 57 Ventoux. Since being discovered, the car has undergone a Concours restoration. *Kay Hottendorff/Ard & Arnoud op de Weegh collection*

car enthusiast, Tristan Veneman. Veneman would have loved to search for the Sleeping Beauties himself, but tragically fell fatally ill in 2002. After Tristan's death, Ard took over the search to find the cars.

During the next four years, father and son op de Weegh mainly came to the same conclusions I had drawn; they knew about Dovaz, the Sleeping Beauties garden, the barn-find museum, and a few restored cars.

Perhaps the op de Weeghs didn't have as much information on single cars as I had because I had compiled all available data into a comprehensive list of the Sleeping Beauties. But Ard and Arnoud had already acquired interesting information I didn't have. Arnoud had convinced his father to travel to the location of the former barn-find museum in the French city of Sarlat in 2006 to find a trail of the cars. They talked to local people, but nobody seemed to know where the cars had gone. After hours of asking, they finally met a man who had talked to a truck driver about the cars 16 years earlier. The truck driver told them he was supposed to deliver his load of cars to an address in a small town nearby in 1984. People in the town told Ard and Arnoud the cars might have been delivered to a nearby castle, but when they arrived at the castle they were told to leave. They believed they were finally onto a hot lead!

Many of the 55 cars still remain in their as-found condition. This 1937 Cord 812 SC Berline is part of a small collection in France, where the owner has decided to preserve the cars as he bought them. *Kay Hottendorff/ Ard & Arnoud op de Weegh collection*

Furthermore, they contacted the original Sleeping Beauties photographer who gave them a 16-minute video showing the cars in their original habitat in 1983. It was an amazing historic document!

When Ard and Arnoud visited me in Northern Germany shortly after Christmas 2006, we decided to share our collective data and create an international joint venture to solve the Sleeping Beauties mystery. This turned out to be a good decision!

Ard was the communications and foreign language expert in our new team. He had unsuccessfully tried to contact Michel Dovaz before and continued to do so by phone, mail, and email. He also employed various contacts in the classical car world. Nothing seemed to work, however, as the man remained a phantom.

I archived our results and analyzed the new material as it came in. The identification of the cars done by various publications turned out to be faulty. The only reliable sources of information we had were the photos and video dating back to the 1980s. Sometimes we had to identify a car from a single rear-view photo partly overgrown with bushes.

Arnoud was our technical specialist and began to compile data on single car types belonging to the collection. His painstaking Internet researches identified Sleeping Beauty cars in general and individual cars in particular.

Even though this intriguing streamlined Tatra 600 Tatraplan was purchased by a new owner, it remains in a setting similar to when it was discovered decades earlier. *Kay Hottendorff/Ard & Arnoud op de Weegh collection*

At this time we felt there had to be more. Some restored cars popped up, but too many cars remained undiscovered. Might some Sleeping Beauties still be asleep to this day?

We decided to follow our hottest lead, the mysterious castle near Sarlat. Did it belong to Michel Dovaz? We looked at aerial photos that identified ìshadowsî in the garden that we suspected were cars. Had they really been stored outdoors another 24 years?

Ard compared voices on different answering machines to find matches between Dovaz's other residences and this castle. He also contacted the registered owner of the castle. This man denied any knowledge of the collection and eventually, annoyed by our questions, threatened to call the police.

To this day, the role of this castle hasn't been solved. It might or might not belong to Michel Dovaz. Later we found out the castle doesnít seem to be as important as we believed in 2007.

In early 2007, I visited an Alfa Romeo Internet forum and found a report of a man who visited Dovaz and his cars at a castle in Southern France back in 1988. This definitely was not the castle near Sarlat, but located more to the south. We needed to find this place! The report had been written by a man from Canada who owned an Alfa Romeo similar to Dovaz's 1948 Alfa Romeo 6C2500 Competizione.

Another museum diorama sets this 1941 Lincoln Continental in a similar scene as when it was shown in the *Automobile Quarterly* story of 1984. *1989–90, Foto Edmund Nankivell*

I managed to gain this man's trust, but after 19 years he didn't remember the name or precise location of the castle. Fortunately, a couple of months later (with some persistent emails from me), my Canadian contact managed to find the castle's name in his old files. The castle was not far from the French city of Montauban. This was definitely a place to visit!

In the meantime, the research for single cars turned up another museum sighting of the Sleeping Beauties. Via a British Jowett Jupiter expert I found out that a car from the Dovaz collection had been sighted in a private French car museum a couple of years earlier. Photos promised there might be even more of the Sleeping Beauties there . . . jackpot!!! Unfortunately the owner didn't answer my English language emails. But no problem: One French language email from Ard and we had an invitation to visit the museum. But did we understand the man's answer correctly . . . he had 10 Sleeping Beauties at his place!?!?

Now the three of us had two good reasons to travel to France: the castle we suspected as being the location of at least part of the collection and the private car museum. By the way: the private car museum was located . . . yes, in another castle. There are lots of them in Southern France!

Arnoud organized a car via his employer, a car dealership, Ard coordinated a date with the gentlemen in France for our visit, and I booked the hotels. Within two weeks the three of us were on the road to France in early

May 2007. On our way south we couldnít resist stopping at the former Dovaz property near Paris to shoot photos of the famous estate that hosted the Sleeping Beauties until 1984. Everything looked like in the earlier photos, but in much better condition and, sadly, without any cars. Nevertheless there was something special in the air. While at the estate, we spoke in whispers, almost as if the spirits of the Sleeping Beauties were still around. A haunting moment for us.

The next day we reached the private car museum. The small castle near the Southern France city of Pomport is surrounded by beautiful landscape amidst vineyards and houses the museum and a winery. After more than 20 years, my high school French was too rusty to exchange more than single words with our host. Thankfully, Ard's French was much better. The castle's owner, a pleasant gentleman, warmly welcomed us and led us to the exhibition room. What we had hoped for during the past weeks became true: The museum housed 10 of the former "Sleeping Beauties" in unrestored condition! This was a really extraordinary discovery.

Among some 25 other unrestored classics, we spotted 8 cars we knew from so many Sleeping Beauties photos: one Bentley, both Cords, the Jowett, one Lincoln, one Lotus, the Panhard & Levassor, and one Rolls-Royce. Even one car we didnít know was there, an Alfa Romeo, which Michel Dovaz had acquired later.

Although unrestored, these cars were in a much better condition than we thought from looking at the 1983 photos. We took lots of photos of the nine Dovaz cars in the museumís display room, but finally began to wonder where the tenth Sleeping Beauty might be. During the welcome our hosts had said something about the "Tatra" being "over there" and had pointed to the vineyard. Might this car still be placed outdoors, like it had been back in 1983? No, much better: Our host led us to a very old stone building nearby. Our hearts nearly stood still when we entered the building. The Tatra 600 Tatraplan, with its distinctive rear dorsal fin, had been placed in an authentic barn-find scene amongst other classics and car parts in an ancient, dusty barn.

The scenario was completely unintended, but strongly reminded us of the 1983 photos taken in the barns of the Sleeping Beauties garden near Paris. This particular Sleeping Beauty goes on sleeping to this day.

During our visit, the castle's owner, a close friend of Dovaz, supplied details on the backgrounds of the collection. In 1984, the cars had been relocated to the castle near Montauban. Publicity and subsequent harassments had been too much for Dovaz after the first Sleeping Beauties press exposure back in 1983. He decided that the only solution was to put the cars on several trucks and relocate them some 400 miles to the south. Some of the cars were put on temporary display in the barn-find museum in Sarlat from 1989 to 1990.

This Sleeping Beauties reunion brings together the people who investigated the real story for years. From left to right, they are Arnoud op de Weegh, Ard op de Weegh, and Kay Hottendorff. The fourth gentleman is Michel Dovaz, known as the mysterious "Pierre" in previous articles, who assembled and owned the collection for decades. *Kay Hottendorff/Ard & Arnoud op de Weegh collection*

By 1990, the collection was dissolved and most of the cars were sold. This hard decision had been made in the dining room of the small castle near Pomport. Some unsold cars were stored in the private car museum of Dovaz's friend in 1990, where 10 still remain to this day. The museum's owner meanwhile acquired two of the Cords, but the others still belong to Michel Dovaz.

After having purchased some wine, we thanked our host for his hospitality and said goodbye. On our way home we made a detour to see the other castle not far from Montauban, which had been the first destination of the 1984 relocation. We found a large and impressive building on a hilltop, a small barn near the street, and a World War II bunker on the backside of the building. Definitely the scenery our contact from Canada had described, but without any cars. Another mystery had been solved.

A few months later, in summer 1997, Ard and Arnoud made contact with the current owner of the most famous Sleeping Beauty, the 1935 Bugatti Type 57 Ventoux depicted in the title photo of the book *Sleeping Beauties* and on the poster I had received in 1997.

Unfortunately I didn't have the time to accompany Ard and Arnoud when they visited the owner of the now completely restored car, a surgeon from

Northern France. At this time my wife and I were expecting our second baby within days. Sometimes there are things more important and more wonderful than chasing old cars, believe it or not.

Meanwhile our list of international contacts and the reputation of our project kept growing. In combination, Arnoud's and my improved Internet research skills led to the discovery of more surviving Sleeping Beauties: Alfa Romeo, Aston Martin, Bugatti, Ferrari, Siata. . . .

In October 2007 a brand-new photo volume based on the 1980s photos allowed me to complete the list of 55 Sleeping Beauties and to create an exact location map of the Sleeping Beauties garden, including the exact placement of every single car (shown in the 1983 status).

That same month Ard had his greatest success. His persistence finally succeeded, and Dovaz answered one of Ard's letters. Time for another journey to France! On November 3, I flew to Paris. Ard and Arnoud drove by car and picked me up at the Champs-Élysées Boulevard near the famous triumphal arch in the middle of Paris. Soon after, we met 79-year-old Michel Dovaz in his nearby residence. We didn't know what to expect, having in mind the somewhat negative descriptions on his person, which we had read about in earlier publications.

The man we found was completely different from our expectations. Dovaz is a hospitable, intelligent, friendly, and self-confident man who was still leading a very active life. The famous wine critic welcomed us with a glass of champagne and talked to us about his former collection and especially the 21 Bugattis he owned throughout his life. During more than three and a half hours, Dovaz openly answered our questions and filled the last gaps in our story.

We had succeeded. We solved the last mysteries of the Sleeping Beauties.

We had made the decision to write a book on the fate of the Sleeping Beauties somewhat earlier but nevertheless it took us another year to do so. With much persuasion, Ard found and convinced a Dutch and later a British publisher to endorse our project. Finally, on November 21, 2008, the Dutch language edition *Het lot van de Slapende Schoonheden* was presented to the public. The English language edition, *The Fate of the Sleeping Beauties*, will follow in autumn 2010 (Veloce Publishing, ISBN 978-1-845840-70-9).

The book covers the complete story of the Sleeping Beauties collection—from 1948 when young Michel Dovaz bought his very first Bugatti, to the moment in 1983 when the famous photos went around the world, to the present—telling the various fates of many of the single Sleeping Beauties.

NOTE: *The Fate of the Sleeping Beauties* will be distributed in the United States by Motorbooks.

CHAPTER FIVE

Prospectors
and Fanatics

The Corvette Sleuth

The inside of Corvette Repair in Valley Stream, New York, looks like almost any other Corvette repair facility: the shop contains new and old Corvettes in various stages of restoration, new body panels being mounted, and cars being painted in the spray booth. In other words, it is a somewhat disorganized but productive space.

If you could look inside the head of owner Kevin Mackay, you'd see one of the most organized, methodical automotive barn-finding minds in the world.

Mackay started Corvette Repair 25 years ago after he became bored with his job as a line mechanic at a Chevrolet dealership.

"I always had a passion for cars," said Mackay, 53. "I was mechanically inclined, so I went from model cars to go karts and mini bikes to Chevys. I figured, what did I have to lose by opening my own business? I was not married, no kids. So I took a gamble and now twenty-five years later, I'm still hunting down old cars."

Corvette Repair is one of the most respected Corvette restoration shops in the industry. They have produced 246 National Corvette Restorers Society (NCRS) Top Flight Award winners, 87 Bloomington Gold winners, and 73 Vette Fest Triple Crown winners.

But hunting down significant Corvettes is what drives Mackay. Listed below are just a couple of the discoveries he's made over the past decade. He has so many stories that I suspect I could fill an entire book with Mackay's Corvette barn finds!

1956 Sebring Corvette

"Corvette built four factory-backed Corvettes that ran at Sebring in 1956," said Mackay. "They were numbers 1, 5, 6, and 7, and the interesting thing about it was that chassis for 1, 5, and 6 were all titled as 1955 Corvettes with prototype 1956 bodies mounted on those chassis. The number 7 car was the only Corvette entered that was titled as a 1956. This was the first year for Corvettes in endurance racing, and they were all painted white with blue stripes. They all had dual quads because fuel injection wasn't available until 1957."

One other Corvette competed at Sebring that year; entry number 3, which was silver blue with a red interior and entered by Carl Beuhler of Chicago.

"Carl bought that car from Dick Doane Chevrolet in Chicago, drove it all the way down to Sebring, raced it, then drove it back home again," said Mackay.

Eagle-eyed barn-finder Kevin Mackay saw this old Sebring photograph of the 1956 Corvette team and tracked down this re-bodied 1955 Corvette (No. 3 on right) through the license plate number check through the DOT. *Kevin Mackay collection*

Beuhler's Corvette finished 23rd overall, having completed 136 laps against the winning Ferrari of Juan Manuel Fangio with 194 laps.

The car competed in the race without issue and was successfully driven back up to Chicago and never seen again. Until Kevin Mackay got on the case.

"A friend of mine, Lauren Lundberg, found a photograph of all the Corvettes that raced in Sebring in 1956," said Mackay. "All the cars are facing forward except for Beuhler's car, which is facing the opposite direction. You could read the license plate: Illinois number 4346.

"Lauren took the plate number to the Department of Motor Vehicles and ran a check. This was before the Privacy Act came into effect in 1992. So he came up with the owner's name and the car's VIN."

It was through this search that Mackay discovered Sebring car number 3, originally owned by a C. Beuhler, was in fact registered and restored in the National Corvette Restorers Society to Top Flight, Certified Gold standards.

When Beuhler returned from Sebring, he brought the car into Dick Doane Chevrolet for service. While it was there, a mechanic drove the car home at night and the dual-quad carburetors flooded. A fire ensued, and the body sustained damage. Beuhler settled for a Mercedes as a trade.

Doane Chevrolet rebodied the car with a brand-new 1955 Corvette body (remember, the cars were titled as 1955 Corvettes). It was sold and vanished.

"The car was disguised all those years as a perfectly restored 1955 Corvette," said Mackay. "I tracked the car down to an owner in Atlanta, and

The No. 3 Corvette (third from left) prior to the start of the 1956 Sebring 12-Hour race. Carl Beuhler drove the car from Chicago to Sebring, raced to a 23rd-place overall finish, and drove the car home to Chicago again. *Kevin Mackay collection*

the guy who owned it said it was for sale for one hundred twenty thousand dollars.

"I figured I'd have to take it all apart, find another '56 body to put on it and then what would it be worth? At the time, maybe three hundred fifty thousand dollars. It wasn't worth it, so I passed on it."

A few years later, though, other significant Corvette race cars, such as the Gulf Oil cars, began selling for more than $1 million, so Mackay decided to pursue the Sebring Corvette once again.

"I called the guy who had it and told him I wanted to buy the car," said Mackay. "He told me it was sold, and I should have bought it three years earlier. I told him I didn't have the money then."

"Well I sold it to a guy near Cartersville, Georgia," the man said.

About that same time, one of Mackay's friends, Phil Schwartz, called and said he'd like to buy an old straight-axle Corvette. "If you find one for me, you can do the restoration on it for me," said Schwartz.

When Mackay told his friend about the 1956 Sebring car, Schwartz said, "Let's get it!"

"Well, I can't," said Mackay.

"Can't? Why?" asked Schwartz.

Mackay told him the story of the missing Sebring car that was probably still somewhere in Georgia.

"He told me to hunt this car real quick; so he ate me alive once a week for six months," said Mackay.

Mackay found out that there is a classic car dealership in Cartersville, and he called that phone number.

"I'm looking for a 1955 Corvette, VIN No. 24. Do you have it for sale?" asked Mackay.

"I had it, but I sold it," said the proprietor. "Why do you want it so bad?"

Mackay made up a story that a customer of his once owned the car and wanted to buy it back again.

"Can I have the new owner's phone number?" asked Mackay. "But the guy wasn't stupid; he wanted to broker the deal."

The proprietor of the classic car sales business called the car's new owner in Texas.

Phone calls went back and forth between Mackay in New York, the classic car business in Georgia, and the Corvette's owner in Texas.

"I said I wanted the car and for him to name his price," said Mackay. "The guy said it could probably be had for one hundred seventy-five thousand dollars. I said, 'Wow, that's kind of steep.'

When Mackay had tracked down the 1955 chassis, it had been re-bodied as a 1955 Corvette, correct for the chassis number but incorrect for the car's amazing history. *Kevin Mackay*

"Then he called me back and said the guy didn't want to sell it. He had a big collection and wanted to keep the car.

"So I gave it one more shot. I said, 'Look, every car has a price; how much will he let the car go for?'"

Mackay wound up paying $190,000 for the car. A king's ransom for a standard 1955 Corvette, but for a Sebring race car, it was still a bargain.

"It will take another two hundred to two hundred fifty thousand dollars to restore that car properly, but that car right now is worth one million dollars plus," he said.

1960 Briggs Cunningham Le Mans Corvette

Corvette race cars are rare, but Corvettes that competed in the 24 Hours of Le Mans are rarer still.

"I started to do my research," said Mackay. "Let's see, four cars were entered in 1960, none in 1961, one in 1962, none in 1963 through 1966, one in 1967, two in 1968, and so on.

"Only sixteen Corvettes competed at Le Mans from 1960 to 1976, so they are very rare. My friend, Ed Mueller of Franklin Lakes, New Jersey, owns the 1967 Corvette that raced at Le Mans, so that leaves fifteen cars that raced there and possibly could still be found.

"So I thought to myself, 'I'm just the man for the job.'"

Mackay is nothing if not ingenious. He went to a New York French school and hired one of the students to write a letter to send to the FIA in France along with a bouquet of flowers.

"I really schmoozed them," he said. "I told them I was starting a race registry concentrating on Corvettes that raced at Le Mans.

"Six months later I received at fax listing all the VIN numbers of the Corvettes that raced there.

"Talk about excitement; I was probably the only guy in the United States who had that information at that time."

Mackay used the VIN numbers and had them cross-referenced with Corvettes registered for the street in the United States. He got two hits: one was VIN No. 2538, which was titled and registered in St. Louis, and the other, VIN No. 4117, was registered in California. But its owner knew of the car's Le Mans history and had restored the car back to racing specs.

So Mackay decided to concentrate on the St. Louis car, which ran in the 1960 race.

Briggs Cunningham, a renowned American sportsman who entered cars at Le Mans for a decade, fielded three Corvettes at the French classic in 1960. The cars, all white with dark blue racing stripes, were numbered 1, 2, and 3. All three cars were ordered with fuel injection from Don Allen Chevrolet in New York City.

"So each car could be identified while racing at night, they were color-coded," said Mackay. "The No. 1 car had white headlight covers and a white light on the roof, the No. 2 car had blue headlight covers and a blue light on the roof, and the No. 3 car had red headlight covers and a red light on the roof.

"I knew the car in St. Louis was either the No. 1 or No. 3 car, because the No. 2 car, which had been driven by Dr. Dick Thompson, had already been discovered in a California junkyard."

Mackay was onto one of the greatest finds of his career.

"I got hold of Bill Walsh in St. Louis, who owned the car," he said. "Thankfully he had no idea what the car was. He just thought it was valuable because it was red with red interior, had a radio delete option, and had a special engine in it.

"But Walsh didn't want to sell it.

"So I got really friendly with him and his wife. Every holiday season I'd send him a Corvette hat, or a Corvette T-shirt, or a Corvette book. And I'd always include a message on the card saying, 'And when you're ready to sell, I'm your man.'"

Using VIN numbers from Le Mans records, Mackay tracked down this proper-looking, restored 1960 Corvette. The VIN numbers, though, told of the Corvette's incredible history as one of Briggs Cunningham's three-car Le Mans 24-Hour team. *Kevin Mackay collection*

When he found the car, Mackay told a couple of friends about the Corvette. "I told them it was just a matter of time before the car was mine," he said.

"The first person I told was my best friend, Chip Miller, co-founder of Carlisle Events in Pennsylvania."

"Kevin," Miller said, "I graduated high school in 1960, and that Corvette was my all-time favorite car. I want that car."

Mackay and Miller shook hands that when he secured the car, Mackay would sell it to his friend.

"I really didn't have that kind of money myself," said Mackay. "So we shook hands and waited."

Miller asked Mackay to call him whenever he got the word that car was theirs.

Another person Mackay told about the car was the original driver of the car, John Fitch. Soon thereafter Fitch happened to mention it to someone when he was being inducted into the Corvette Museum Hall of Fame. Within a couple days, Mackay was getting calls from car collectors all over the United States.

"People started lining up to buy a car I didn't even own yet," said Mackay.

Mackay waited and waited. Finally, seven years after his first phone call, he called Mr. and Mrs. Walsh to wish them happy holidays, and he got a glimmer of hope from Mrs. Walsh.

"Thank you, Kevin, for the thoughtful gifts," she said. "I've been telling my husband for so long to sell you that car."

"I apologized for being a pest, but I just wanted to let them know I was passionate about the car," said Mackay. "I never mentioned the words Cunningham or Le Mans to them. I just mentioned Corvette.

"It turns out that Mr. Walsh had back pain in his advanced age, and his wife convinced him to sell it. She told him they could buy a new Lincoln Navigator if he sold me the Corvette.

"So one day he calls and leaves me a voicemail saying, 'I've decided I'm going to sell you the car.'

"I looked at the clock, and it was 1 a.m. But Chip said to call whenever the deal happened, so I called him."

Ring, ring, ring, ring . . .

"Hello," said a sleepy Miller.

"Chip, I got the car," said Mackay. "So he starts yelling to his wife, 'Judy, he got the car. Kevin got me the car!'"

A reasonable price was agreed on, and money was transferred by wire.

"Considering the car's value, we stole it," said Mackay.

When the Corvette arrived in his Long Island restoration shop in 2000, Mackay gave the car a careful appraisal. He could see the impression in the fiberglass where the fuel filler neck had been installed for Le Mans. He could see the additional lighting in the back, and the brake scoops and ducting was still in place.

"This car had virgin fiberglass," he said. "All the panels that were on the car when it raced in 1960 were still on the car."

Instead of dismantling the car himself, he decided to bring in 14 experts from around the United States for the weekend to assist in the process of dissecting the car for restoration.

"We had people from General Motors; we had straight-axle Corvette experts; we had two of the original drivers who hadn't seen the car since they raced it in 1960, John Fitch and Bob Grossman.

"We even had a professional video crew to document the whole process," he said.

"The first thing we checked was the body for damage. After the dust cleared, we realized we had the No. 3 Le Mans car. We knew that the No. 1 car caught fire and the passenger side of the nose on the No. 2 car had been damaged. But this car had a virtually perfect front end, which meant it was the class winner."

Le Mans inspection records made identifying the car confusing. Inspectors mixed up the VIN numbers on the No. 2 (2438) and No. 3 (4117) Corvettes, but inspecting the body in Mackay's shop confirmed the mix-up.

"We completely gutted that car," he said. "Seven guys dismantled and documented it in seven hours down to the bare glass. We stripped the interior and trim off the car step by step."

Still, the fact that one of the Cunningham Corvettes cannot be found bothers Mackay.

"The No. 1 car can't be found," he said. "I have the VIN number, but I can't find it. I can trace it up to 1974, when it was last registered for the street in a Tampa, Florida, area apartment complex. I've walked up and down streets in Tampa, knocking on doors, but I can't find the car. If I only had x-ray vision to look through garage walls.

"I've even thought about hiring a psychic to help me find the car. I mean, how many times have you heard on these TV stories about a psychic finding a lost child? I'm at the point with that car that I'm going to find the best psychic I can to help me find that car.

"If it's still out there."

Notes

• Chip Miller passed away from complications of amyloidosis, a rare form of cancer, in 2004. The No. 3 Cunningham Corvette remains owned by his estate.
• One of the Corvette experts who attended the dismantling of the Cunningham Corvette was renowned California collector Bruce Meyer. Meyer expressed his interest in acquiring the car, but Miller wasn't interested in selling it. So Mackay located and purchased Cunningham No. 2 for Meyer. At one time, that Corvette resided in a California junkyard. At last word, all parties were pleased with the results.

The Rebel Corvette

"I was at a swap meet in Mahwah, New Jersey, at Ramapo College," said Mackay. "It's an annual event and I try to go to all of them.

"While I was there, I started looking through a stack of old magazines this guy had for sale. I came across a *Corvette Corner* magazine, and on the cover was this Corvette race car with a Rebel paint job."

Mackay opened up and read the story. It was a 1969 Corvette with the rare L88 engine option that was ordered by Orlando Costanza of Tampa and raced at Sebring from 1969 to 1973.

The Rebel Corvette, with the rare 1969 L88 engine option, finished eighth overall in the 1972 24 Hours of Daytona, which that year was shortened to six hours in an effort to increase fan base. Drivers Bob Johnson and Dave Heinz finished first in class for the 2500cc GT category. *Kevin Mackay collection*

"I said to myself, 'What a neat car to find.' So I called telephone information and got Costanza's phone number in about thirty seconds.

"I called him and told him I just read about his old race car in a magazine and wanted to learn a little more about the car. He told me he had the original paperwork and pictures of the car, but he had sold the car to a father and son racing team, Toye and Dana English."

Mackay contacted the English family and was told they had sold the car to a Mr. Alex Davidson in New York. He called Davidson.

"I'm from New York too," I said. "Where are you?

"He was up near Syracuse. He knew he had once owned the Rebel Corvette, but nobody cared back then. They weren't classy or desirable; they were just yesterday's race cars.

"I have a passion for these L88 Corvettes because they only made one hundred sixteen of them in 1969. Knowing that this car in 1972 was a class winner at both Daytona and Sebring was unbelievable. You talk about an investment; this car was a no-brainer to me. It was better than real estate."

Mackay figured he was already well on the way to tracking down the Rebel Corvette. After all, he had already contacted the first, second, and third owners, so he figured he was halfway there.

Davidson didn't remember who he sold the car to. He said, "Kevin, it was a guy in North Carolina or South Carolina, I don't remember. And I think he was a doctor. I'll think about it and you can call me back."

Every six months or so Mackay called Davidson. One time it seemed that Davidson was getting a little bit testy. "Look, I gave you all the information I have," he said. "He was a doctor in the Carolinas, and I think his name was Charlie. Don't call me anymore."

OK, so Mackay learned one more clue: his name was Charlie.

He called the SCCA and spoke to historian Harry Hanley. "Harry, I need your help," said Mackay. "I'm looking for a doctor with the name Charles who raced a Corvette in the Southeast in the 1970s."

Hanley called a week later with some good news. "I got one hit," said Hanley. "His name is Charles West, and he's a dentist."

Mackay was on the hunt. He called information, got the phone number for Dr. West's office and talked to his secretary.

"Can I please speak to Dr. West," said Mackay. "I'd like to talk to him about a racing Corvette."

In about thirty seconds, he was on the phone.

West was older and had retired from racing. But he was a big car guy and collected all kinds of old race cars. And he still owned the Corvette. It was stored in a junkyard that he owned.

And it wasn't for sale.

"I asked if I could come and look at the car, and he said no problem," said Mackay. "He said he hadn't laid his eyes on it for years. I told him I'd be flying down to Atlanta in a few weeks and it wouldn't be too long a trip to drive up to his hometown in Greenwood, South Carolina."

"What day do you want to come?" asked Dr. West.

"Saturday evening," Mackay told him. "He told me he had a wedding that evening that wouldn't be over until eleven p.m. I told him no problem, that I would be there waiting for him."

Mackay met Dr. West in the parking lot of the wedding reception. Dr. West was dressed in his tuxedo, and Mrs. West was in a gown.

"He climbs into his pickup truck and we drive a few miles toward the junkyard," said Mackay. "I had been on pins and needles for weeks I was so excited. I hadn't slept right."

Dr. West climbed out of the truck in his tux, but his wife called for him to put on his overalls. He did; then he and Mackay marched in the darkness toward the back of the lot.

"I was loaded up like a Boy Scout with flashlights," he said.

"Kevin, I think it's over there somewhere," said West. "I remember I had a

After sitting for decades under a deteriorated blue tarp in South Carolina, this ragged-looking race car was surprisingly intact, down to its "1970 Corvette Le Mans Race Team" decal on the back window. *Kevin Mackay collection*

big blue tarp over it."

So Mackay walked over to a blue tarp, grabbed it, and lifted. As soon as he did, though, the tarp was so brittle it disintegrated in his hands.

"I looked at the car," said Mackay. "It still had Alex Davidson's name on the door. I thought to myself, 'I can't believe this; it's the old Rebel Corvette I saw on the magazine cover.'"

The car had no engine and had been sitting there since the 1970s.

"One thing I noticed was a decal on the back window that said 1970 Corvette Le Mans Race Team," he said. "If you look at the cover of *Corvette Corner* in 1972, you can see that decal there.

"But it never went to Le Mans, even though it was invited. After the car had won its class at Daytona and Sebring, it was too worn out to be prepared and shipped out to France."

Mackay also noticed the original interior was still in the car from 1972, as was the steering wheel, the control panel, seat, seat belts, roll bar, and even the milk box that held the battery in place. But the body was beaten up because it sat outside for so many years.

"I needed to own that car, so I started talking to the doctor about what it would take to own it," said Mackay. "He saw my passion, and I told him I really wanted this car.

"He said that he wanted to buy back his old Porsche race car, and if I paid for that car, I could have his Corvette. I asked how much the Porsche was, and he said $7,000. I told him I had $1,000 in my wallet and that I would be back within a week to pick it up."

Mackay said this is one of the most significant American race cars in history. It was the only C3 Corvette to win at Daytona and Sebring the same year.

Interestingly, the Rebel Corvette also raced on Goodyear radial tires in 1972 and 1973.

The Rebel Corvette offered a unique rivalry to the racing Corvette of John Greenwood, which featured an American flag paint scheme.

"To poke fun at Greenwood, they painted Rebel flags in the car," said Mackay. "Greenwood was the car to beat, so the Rebel paint job was like slapping John in the face. It was exciting; like the Civil War was being battled out on the racetrack."

Mackay restored the car and kept it for about ten years. He eventually sold it to collector and vintage racer Larry Bowman of California.

Baldwin-Motion Phase III Corvette

"You hear these stories all the time," said Mackay. "I used to own this and I used to own that; I never should have sold it. Most of the time they're just full of hot air."

Mackay thought his longtime friend Phil Schwartz was weaving a tall tale when he said he owned a brand-new Baldwin-Motion Phase III Corvette when he graduated from high school.

Then one day he walked into Mackay's shop with a photograph of himself standing next to the car.

"Holy crap," said Mackay. "I guess you were telling the truth for the last twenty-five years!"

"What did you think, I was bullshitting you?" asked Schwartz.

"OK, so where is it?" asked Mackay.

"I don't know," said Schwartz. "I did very well in school, so my dad told me I could buy any car I wanted. I read all the magazines and read about the Baldwin-Motion Corvettes and thought it was the coolest thing on the planet. And it was built right here on Long Island, so my dad said, 'Get it.' I had an open checkbook."

This is a rare car. Mackay said that only about 12 Motion Phase III Corvettes were ever built.

"Phil, you've got to find your old car," said Mackay. "Wouldn't it be great to be reunited with your old car forty years later?"

Mackay's friend Phil Schwartz received this Baldwin-Motion Phase III Corvette as a high school graduation gift in 1969. He sold it in 1970 and has regretted ever since. After several attempts, he finally did repurchase the car almost four decades later. Mackay is now restoring if for his friend. *Phil Schwartz*

Schwartz explained that the only reason he sold it after one year of ownership was because he got married very young. He wanted to start a family, so the two-seater sports car had to go. He sold it in 1970 to a guy in Queens.

"I asked him if he had any documentation, and he said he didn't," said Mackay. "Who cared back then; it was just an old hot rod."

But Schwartz started to rattle off some facts about the car. It was orange, had factory side pipes, and was the only Baldwin Corvette that was ordered with power windows and leather interior.

So one day Mackay was on eBay and started to search for "Baldwin-Motion," "Motion Performance," and "Baldwin Chevrolet."

"An unrestored orange Corvette comes up without documentation," he said. "I called Phil and said, 'Guess what? You're not going to believe this, but there is an orange Baldwin-Motion Corvette on eBay.'"

"You got to be kidding me," said Schwartz.

Schwartz hung up and signed onto eBay. He called Mackay back.

"That's my car," said Schwartz.

"How do you know?" asked Mackay.

"You see that gauge mounted on the cowl?" asked Schwartz. "That's a Stewart-Warner fuel gauge. I mounted that myself. And see those ladder bars under the car? I painted them that way.

"I bet if you call that guy right now, he'd tell you it has power windows and leather interior."

The problem was that the Buy-It-Now price was $225,000; much more than Schwartz was willing to pay for his old car.

Mackay called the owner, who was a Connecticut state trooper.

"You want to end that auction right now?" asked Mackay. "My guy will give you one hundred fifty thousand dollars for it."

"No, I'm riding out the auction," said the trooper.

"So I asked him about the interior," he said. "He said it was leather and had power windows. And he told me the gauge on the cowl was a Stewart-Warner fuel gauge.

"So I called Phil. 'It's your car.' Phil starts freaking out. 'Get me the damn car,' he said.

"I called the trooper back, and he said two hundred twenty-five thousand dollars or nothing. Phil said he would only pay one hundred fifty thousand dollars. So I watched the car be sold to someone else."

When the auction was over, Mackay called the trooper. He sold it and wouldn't identify the new owner's name, address, or the car's VIN number.

"I called Phil," he said. "You lost the car. You snooze and you lose.

"Phil told me for twenty-five years that he wanted that car, and he lost it again.

"So after another couple of years of torture, he calls me back. 'Kevin, I'm sick over this thing. I can't take this money with me. Please find me my car again.'"

One day Mackay was on the Yenko.net website and they were having a big auction up in Connecticut. As part of the inventory was an orange Baldwin-Motion Corvette.

"Phil, I found your car again," he said. "It's on the Yenko website. They're having an auction this weekend."

"I'm going to a wedding this weekend," said Schwartz.

"OK, so you'll lose the car again," said Mackay. "So he cancels his wedding plans and we leave at six a.m. Saturday morning to drive up to Connecticut for the auction."

There was no reserve on the car, but it was the nicest car of the 80 or so being auctioned that day. Schwartz was sweating. Mackay was getting nervous he'd blow his cool.

"Phil, stay away from that car," said Mackay. "And keep your trap shut.

"In fact, I needed to stay away from that car as well, because I'm too well-known in the area, so if people see me, the price will go up."

The new owner of the car apparently had some issues with the IRS and needed to sell all his cars. He did confirm that the car was purchased from the Connecticut state trooper. But now the car was restored, and according to Mackay, it was a poor job.

"The auction was going slow: five thousand, ten thousand, fifteen thousand dollars," said Mackay. "Phil said he was too nervous to bid, so I took his bidder's pass and sat right up in front so everyone could see me. I wasn't going to lose this car.

"Phil told me to stay on it and he'd tell me when to cap it off. 'Don't lose that car,' he said."

The bidding goes up to $100,000 then slows. Mackay begins thinking that this is good and that he'll get the car for $100,000. Then bidding begins again: $110,000, $120,000, $130,000, $140,000, $150,000, $160,000, $170,000.

"Phil says to stay in it," said Mackay.

"It goes to one hundred eighty thousand, then one hundred ninety thousand dollars," he said. "So I walk over to the other guy who's bidding in the back of the room. I tell him, 'Whatever it takes, this car is mine. So if you want to bid it up, go ahead.'

"He said, 'Get out of here, I want the car.'"

$200,000!

The other guy backed out and Mackay secured the car for his friend.

"Don't you say a word until you pay for the car and take care of the paperwork. Then you can tell people about the car," said Mackay. "In about ten minutes he comes back and starts telling people that he bought this car new forty years ago."

They made a big announcement that the original owner for 1969 bought his old car back.

"Phil still has the same wife, three grown kids, and now he has his old car back," said Mackay. "We're restoring the car exactly back to the way it was when he was a kid, Cherry Bomb mufflers and everything."

The Snipe Hunter

By Harold Pace

A common rite of passage for many rural youngsters is to be taken on a "snipe hunt." The gullible newcomer is given a bag and a flashlight and left in the woods at night to catch the mythical bird. In truth, there are no snipes to be found anywhere near the site. The point of the charade is to abandon the victim in the cold darkness until he realizes he has been tricked and returns, humiliated, to the campfire for a round of heckling. Of course, there is always the off-chance he will return with SOMETHING alive in the bag, much to the surprise of the conspirators!

Geoff Hacker has been the king of automotive snipe hunters for the past three years, bringing back to life dozens of rare and historically interesting cars that most enthusiasts either never knew existed or had written off as extinct.

How esoteric are the cars Hacker pursues? He currently has both Omohundros and all three El Tiburons known to survive. A Quincy-Lyn Urbacar, a Grantham Stardust, and a Jones Meteor also reside at his Florida home, along with a *Road & Track* Le Mans Coupe, an Allied Cisitalia replica, a Victress S4, and the sole surviving example of the Triplex Chicagoan. Not to forget the Gougeon streamliner, a Maverick-Cadillac, and the Cheetah (AKA Moon) race car transporter (found using *The Cobra in the Barn*). If you don't recognize any of these marques, don't feel bad. Hacker owns four or five cars that even he hasn't identified yet! Although he relishes finding rare cars languishing in garages and barns, the part that Hacker really digs is hunting down the enterprising men and women who created limited-production and one-off cars in the 1940s and 1950s.

Hacker's burning desire to research unique autos was kindled when he met Jon Gruel, who had founded an Internet site devoted to the LaDawri kit cars of the 1950s. Hacker was looking for information on his El Tiburons, beautiful streamlined sports cars built in very small numbers in the early 1960s. The more Hacker talked to other classic specialty car enthusiasts, the more he heard the same stories: almost all of the old kit and specialty cars were gone, and the people who had built them were all dead. But Hacker decided to turn those assumptions on their heads.

"I wasn't finding anything. I was looking for history, not for cars, but I wasn't finding much. Then I changed my approach, to assume that the cars and people were all still out there somewhere, waiting to be found. Then I started finding them." Hacker has a PhD in Industrial Organizational Psychology and teaches college courses online. With that background he was prepared to

Looking like the bird that just ate the fiberglass canary, collector Geoff Hacker of Tampa, Florida, has amassed the largest collection of limited-production sports cars in the world. He owns about 30 cars, at least 5 of which have not yet been identified. *Harold Pace*

wage a systematic search, so he made lists of cars he was interested in finding out more about, based on his interest in rare specialty sports cars, futuristic "teardrop" cars, and sports customs of the 1940s and 1950s. Next he looked for any clues he could find from old magazine articles and cars that came up for sale on eBay. Using simple online search software he tracked down surviving figures from limited-edition car history, who in turn provided leads to find their friends and coworkers.

Within a year Hacker had contacted the family of LaDawri founder Les Dawes, Victress principal Merrill Powell, Glasspar founder Bill Tritt, Sabre salesman Ed Almquist, Allied racer Bill Burke, and many others. Hacker ran down Bangert builder Noel Bangert, even though he had changed his name to Noel Marshall after becoming a Hollywood producer. Meteor kit car maven Dick Jones is now a friend and still has the final Meteor body hanging in his garage. And the Grantham family was not only thrilled to hear about Hacker's Stardust, they turned him onto the only surviving example of a short run of Granthams built in the 1970s. In the course of meeting the founding fathers of the American specialty car industry, he also came across a large number of cars for sale. And since he was interested in classes of cars that were generally underappreciated, he found he could buy many of them for bargain prices. The

Tip of the iceberg: Hacker's driveway at home is like a constantly changing museum of unusual and unidentifiable cars. *Left to right:* Cheetah Transporter; 1946 Kurtis Omohundro Comet; 1937 Goudeon Streamliner; and a 1965 Covington Tiburon Roadster. *Geoff Hacker*

ones he didn't buy he tried to hook up with owners he knew would give them a good home.

Hacker was so impressed with the pioneer car builders he met that he wanted to get them the recognition they deserved. As he began crisscrossing the country on car-finding trips, he'd spend months on the road visiting and interviewing friends he had met on the phone or online, ranging from famed customizer Gene Winfield to race car fabricator Don Edmunds, flathead expert Vern Tardell and dozens of others. As he collected each new car, he also searched out the men and women who built it.

Soon his activities came to the attention of movers and shakers in the car show community. For the last four years he has been involved in the Amelia Island Concours, both as an entrant and an organizer. In 2007 he rounded up enough vehicles for a special Fiberglass Sports Car Class. He has also helped locate classic specialty cars for the Barrington and Palo Alto Concourses, while his own cars have been displayed at the Petersen Automotive and NHRA museums.

Although Hacker has bought and sold dozens of cars, he doesn't consider himself a dealer. He's far more interested in uncovering history than in adding another car to his collection. However, there were a few cars that he REALLY

This is the coupe version of the Covington Tiburon. The coupes were powered by Porsche 356 drivetrains, and the roadsters had Renault R-8 and R-10 mechanicals. *Geoff Hacker*

wanted to find. The first was the Kurtis-Omohundro, one of two custom sports car designed by Indy legend Frank Kurtis and built by his business partner Paul Omohundro in 1947. Hacker first heard of them in 2007, when friend Phil Fleming told him about a pair of lovely sports cars he had seen when he was in school. When Hacker saw Fleming's old photos it set off an alarm in his memory . . . he had recently heard about a similar "mystery car" from its owner, who didn't know what it was. He put the two parts of the puzzle together and realized he had found the first Kurtis-Omohundro, quite possibly the first American postwar sports car! The owner was anxious for it to go to a good home, so Hacker soon took possession. In 2009 it won the "Most Elegant Car" award at the Amelia Island Concours, cheered on by Phil Fleming, whom Hacker had brought along. The surviving Omohundro family members were in attendance later when the car was placed on exhibit at the Petersen Automotive Museum. It took another year to hunt down the second Omohundro. After protracted negotiations it, too, found its way to his house. They are the crown jewels of his collection.

An unrequited love affair with Buckminster Fuller's Dymaxion led to the purchase of a teardrop-shaped car built in the late 1930s by Ronald Gougeon in Bay City, Michigan. It had come up on eBay, but failed to meet even a modest

One of Hacker's favorites is this 1947 Kurtis-Omohundro Comet, one of two built in Los Angeles by the legendary race car builder Frank Kurtis. Hacker owns both. *Geoff Hacker*

reserve. Hacker jumped on it. Based on prewar Ford running gear, it fulfilled Hacker's dream of owning a "car of the future" like the ones illustrated on the cover of 1930s magazines portraying their vision for the twenty-first century (when cities would be covered by giant bubbles and smiling commuters would be zinging along highways suspended in space). Hacker found the Gougeon in 2008 and is currently restoring it with the help of friends met on the Jalopy Journal (H.A.M.B.) website.

Hacker is generous in his praise of the friends who have helped him find both cars and their automotive pioneers. In particular, he singles out Rick D'Louhy, who has ridden along on many of his endeavors and has even bought several of the cars Hacker has found in his travels. In particular, D'Louhy is proud of his prototype Warrior, a one-off mid-engined sports car built in Texas in 1964. It was patterned after the Ford Mustang show car and features a Ford V-4 engine. D'Louhy also ended up with the Bearcage, an unfinished sports-racer started by Don Edmunds for Bill Stroppe. An aluminum-bodied beauty, many of the design concepts from the Bearcage were to be re-used when Edmunds later built the Cheetahs for Bill Thomas.

Hacker has also been instrumental in putting kit car pioneers back into the cars they built so long ago. The Dawes family hadn't thought about the LaDawri

Hacker stores about 10 of his excess fiberglass projects on a friend's farm near his Tampa home, which he refers to as the Fiberglass Farm. *Left to right:* an unidentifiable VW-powered dune buggy CRV/Piranha body and an unknown Ford flathead–powered sports car Hacker calls the Blowfish Car. *Geoff Hacker*

Two more occupants of Fiberglass Farm. *Left to right:* 1956 Byers' Special, which appeared on the cover of the February 1957 *Road & Track* and was named the World's Most Beautiful Sports Car; and a Victress S4. *Geoff Hacker*

114

kit cars since father Les Dawes stopped building them in the mid-1960s. But when Hacker contacted Les' widow, Joan, she was thrilled to know there were still LaDawris both running and much admired by their owners. Within months of making contact, Joan Dawes and her daughter Debra were guests of honor at Amelia Island and took a parade lap around the grounds in a restored LaDawri! It wasn't long before the Dawes family had a LaDawri of their own again. Ditto for Victress founder Merrill Powell and his wife, Gerianne, who now have a pair of Victress C3 coupes, thanks to Hacker's help. Noted race car collector Mark Brinker wound up with a famous Ardun-powered Glasspar after a three-cornered trade engineered by his friend Hacker.

So what does the future hold? Hacker and Gruel have recently set up a website for classic kit car fans called www.forgottenfiberglass.com, and Hacker is working on a book with Rick D'Louhy on the same subject. And he still has a list of cars and people he would like to find. He's proven that interesting, obscure cars are still out there, hiding in barns, dilapidated garages, and cornfields across America, and Hacker intends to find them all!

The Road to
Preservation

by Steve Katzman

Early on the morning of August 17, 2008, my wife, Jeanne, and I arrived in our Aurelia Spider for the Pebble Beach Concours d'Elegance. That trip was inspired by an idle conversation some 25 years earlier.

In the 1980s, a friend and I had been discussing cars that we lusted after. When I mentioned a Lancia Fulvia Zagato, me friend told me about a retired coworker who owned an old Lancia. The man became a recluse and wouldn't talk to anybody. I couldn't have afforded to purchase the car, so I filed the name in my head and let it go.

My friend's story gnawed at me over the years. I ended up digging through phone books at the library, like a prospector trying to trace color up the creek to the mother lode, until they yielded an address and a phone number.

Some years later, I found myself hopping a chainlink fence across a steep gravel driveway. Knocking on the door of a ramshackle house in a little canyon near San Francisco, I was greeted by a rumpled old cowboy. My letters had gone unanswered, but when I'd called, his reserve softened a bit. He told me his car wasn't a coupe—it was an open car. He couldn't remember the model. My curiosity piqued, I'd stayed in touch and eventually was granted an audience. Face to face, Henry and I hit it off right away, but he made it clear the Lancia wasn't for sale. When he had finally found true love, his sweetheart had developed dementia. Broken-hearted, he never married or had children and intended to leave the car to his nephews. No matter, automotive archaeology is its own reward.

I followed him back down the driveway, littered with old gallon jugs, past derelict baby Caterpillar tractors, an old cement truck, and various rusty hulks, only some of which I could identify. As he peeled back the barn doors, I stood there, slack-jawed. There, in all its filthy glory, was an Aurelia Spider.

Henry had been born and raised near Mandan, North Dakota, where his father had a "stoop" coal mine. That's just what it sounds like, and Henry was at least 6 feet 2 inches; the coal mine didn't work too well for him. He told me stories of the most horrendous snowstorms and claimed if he died without ever seeing snow again, he'd die happy. On that count, at least, he succeeded. World War II provided him an exit. After suffering a collapsed lung in basic training, he ended up in the San Francisco Bay Area, working as an instrument maker in support of the war effort. Postwar affluence enabled him to indulge

Henry Teppo (pictured) bought this Lancia Sport Zagato new in 1956 after wrecking his Jaguar XK120. After accumulating 22,000 miles with it, commuting, and participating in sports car events in the San Francisco area, he parked the here in 1963. It was unearthed by Steve Katzman 35 years later. *Steve Katzman*

an interest in cars that dated back to his childhood when he messed with old Chevrolets back in Mandan. Henry's and his friends' car of choice at first was the Hudson Hornet, but in 1954, when they realized that British Motor Cars in San Francisco would take their Hudsons in on trade, they made the move from American iron to British.

He bought the Spider new in late 1956. At that time, he was working as a machinist at the "Rad Lab" (now the Lawrence Berkeley National Laboratory). The Jaguar XK120 he purchased new two years earlier—his first new car—had been tail-ended the day he mailed his last payment, and it was never quite right again. So when BMC offered him $3,500 in trade against the $5,500 for the Lancia, he drove the Spider home. He never really raced it, but drove it in club events (he belonged to the Tyred Wheel Motor Car Club), as well as using it as his commuter. It still carries its Rad Lab parking stickers. After putting less than 22,000 miles on the odometer, mechanical issues led to it being parked in the barn. That act of devotion spared it the fate of all the rest of the automotive carcasses scattered around his ranch.

We kept in touch, and I visited him several times a year. His favorite visits seemed to be when I brought him a plate of Jeanne's Christmas cookies. He still had a machine shop, located in a semi trailer next to his house and an adjoining aluminum teardrop trailer. He also had barns full of various collections. He repaired old radios and had plans to push a road up to the ridge on his property and build an observatory.

One year later, however, I found Henry had been admitted to the hospital, terminally ill. During that time, his house had been burglarized and stripped of copper wire, by, he told me, those same nephews. Upon learning of this, he wanted to make sure the Lancia would go to safe hands. I was to be its caretaker. Henry named his price and told me I could pay when and how I pleased. But as of that moment, the car was mine. As it was midwinter, though, I'd have to wait for the ground to dry out in late spring before I could move things out of the way and extract it.

When Henry passed away only a few months later, I wasted no time getting it out of his barn. It took me a day to clear a path through the barn, and the next day I came back with a flatbed truck. Three more hours to move it the last 25 feet, and the Lancia was safe.

So there in my driveway sat the Spider. A thorough cleaning showed it to be in good shape, though the motor was frozen from sitting in a barn for 30 years, and rodents had taken up residence.

Art, artifacts, and antiques: wear and patina tell a story and are very much a valued part of these objects. But this concept—conservation rather than restoration—is rarely applied to cars. At first merely determined to keep the original paint, a beautiful period pastel green, I found myself ever more committed to saving the original finishes. Factory markings were preserved or replicated where necessary. Most period changes were retained, especially the carburetor linkage made by Bill Breeze, a contemporary of Phil Hill and one of the people who laid out the original Pebble Beach road course. After a major shunt in 1951 he quit racing, but continued to run the Sports Car Center in Sausalito, California, near our home.

The next five years were spent preparing the Spider to return to the road in as authentic a condition as possible. After 30 years in a barn, the motor was frozen solid, the brakes perished, and the fuel tank wickedly foul. A full mechanical recommisioning would be required. NOS pistons and liners were a special find, but many parts had to be fabricated. Though I did almost all the work myself, many friends contributed to the effort, and there's no way I could have done it without their enthusiastic help. In May 1997 I hit the ignition key, and Spider B24S-1117 cranked back into life for the first time since 1963. As it fired, the last acorns and bay nuts blew out of the exhaust pipe in a huge cloud of smoke and dust. For the next nine years we averaged 1,000 miles a year between reunions, club events, and the Monterey weekend. Over and through the snow-covered Sierras to the high deserts, up and down the coast, in the blazing sun and the bitterly cold fog, it's been a reliable companion and has never let us down.

Though we had been considering missing Monterey in 2008, Lancia was to be one of the featured marques at Pebble Beach, so an invitation to bring the Spider certainly changed our minds. With all the chips, stains and dings, dry and cracked leather, and somewhat pitted chrome, the joke had been that all the preparation the car needed was a dusting, but in truth a bit more was required. Aside from fitting a few original pieces, it needed some deferred maintenance. Fresh brake linings and clutch disc were fitted, a coolant leak resolved, hoses checked and replaced as needed, Italian hose clamps replaced American ones, and countless other small items attended to. I declined to scrub the engine and engine compartment and left in the modern electric fuel pump, as it was a driven car. Last, I left the worn tires, then washed but didn't wax it, as I didn't want the car too shiny. Nature abhorring a vacuum, it should come as no surprise that I finished preparation with just days to spare. It's amazing the amount of time it takes to make it look like you've done nothing.

We arrived in time for the Pebble Tour on the Thursday prior to the Concours. Though a seemingly flawless level of preparation was expected of all the cars, the effect was nearly overwhelming. Humbled that our less-than-spotless Spider was included among those fantastic cars, it was then we realized just how right our friends had been when they told us we'd won just by being invited. The sights and sounds of all those different cars, appearing and disappearing along the misty tour route, were fantastic. When was the last time you had to help push start a Lancia D24 sports racer? Over the next few days more and more friends appeared, drawn like moths to a flame, one even taking a redeye flight from the East Coast just to be with us as we showed the Spider the next day. And all weekend long, people kept asking us if we'd *really* driven our "Pebble Car" to Pebble.

So there we were on that overcast show morning, out the door before light, heading for the 18th fairway at Pebble Beach in mist so heavy it may as well have been raining. A half-hour later as we were sitting in line waiting to get in, a prewar Maserati GP car was spitting oil on the Spider's nose with every blip of the throttle. Escorted down the fairway to our spot in Postwar Preservation, I toweled off the windscreen and only then mounted the wipers. The rest of the car was wiped down, the seat belts straightened, the trunk emptied, and that was about it.

That finished, we started to wander the field, eager to feast our eyes on the bounty at hand, but we didn't get far before being called back to the car, as the judges were getting close. After introductions, I had five minutes to present the car, and then they spent another ten minutes looking it over and asking

Performing a thorough cleanup and mechanical upgrade, the unrestored Lancia was awarded second place in the Preservation Class at the 2008 Pebble Beach Concours. Katzman's Lancia was one of the only cars that was actually driven—not trailered—to the event. *Edd Ellison*

questions. The FIVA judges followed shortly behind. And then, after all the months of preparation, all the buildup, the judging was over.

We spent the next few hours looking at cars, many of which we'd only heard or seen pictures of, and talking to friends old and new. After lunch, as the afternoon awards ceremonies proceeded, the air of anticipation increased. By that point, perhaps because of all the splendor on the grass, we had a bit of a "we have a nice car, but . . ." feeling. When the Ferrari next to us was chosen to go to the podium, we were glad for them. When as a finalist we were asked to join them, following a Delahaye, we could hardly believe it.

The three cars were lined up side by side. When the Delahaye on our right was called up for third place, Jeanne and I looked at each other in shock. The next minute we were called up for second in class, and as the Spider climbed the podium, the world first grew large, and then fell away. I don't think I heard a thing the master of ceremonies said. I was gone. By the time we got back down the fairway, our friends were waiting to help us celebrate, and the champagne was a delightful addition to our already ebullient mood. As we enjoyed our little victory, the fields began to thin, and we finally made our way back to our motel one last time.

All that evening and over the next few days, it continued to sink in. Our shoestring project had been recognized as worthy. More importantly, it had been especially appreciated for having been conserved in usable and reliable condition. My intention had never been to make it a "show" car, but rather to represent an honest example of a car of its time that we could use and that also acknowledged its history. One other point I've kept in mind is that as one of two known unrestored Spiders in the world (the other is in Italy), it serves as a benchmark to measure others against, so there is a responsibility to maintain it as-is. A restored car is not necessarily authentic.

Even twelve years ago, in 1998, when we first brought out the Spider, many people thought that an old car should be repainted, rechromed, etc. It was at times comical to watch Jeanne send packing the gold-chained hordes who wanted to buy the car and restore it "the way it ought to be." On the whole, however, we've taken it as an opportunity to educate and advance our point of view. We've seen attitudes change (the inclusion of a Preservation Class at Pebble and other shows is a clear indication of that), and where once we were seen as odd and aesthetically challenged, we now are commended for not ruining the car and are even rewarded. We truly are on the road to preservation.

The Lost Motor Trend
Victress S1A Special

By Guy Dirkin

In 1951, Doc Boyce Smith dreamed of a Victress in every garage. In just a few short years, Doc and his partner Merrill Powell had created the first powerhouse company for fiberglass-bodied American sports cars. Thanks to their efforts, anyone who wanted to, could build themselves their own sports car dream.

This story is about finding and resurrecting a Victress S1A that was hiding in plain sight in the Northwest. What we ultimately found was a car that was part of the early history of postwar American sports cars.

My first knowledge of this particular Victress S1A special was a phone call from my friend Dr. Geoff Hacker, a sports car researcher from Tampa, Florida. I first met Geoff when he contacted me about my Byers SR-100. Geoff has been researching postwar American sport cars and had volumes of information at his fingertips.

During Geoff's research, he had come across tales of a Victress S1A in the Northwest. No one had a picture; just two clues . . . the Northwest Victress had two hood scoops and was rumored to have been in a fire.

The Victress S1A roadster is a beautiful car. Doc Boyce Smith and Hugh Jorgensen designed this car in 1951, as they said in their own words, "to out-Jag the Jaguar XK120." Turn the front grille sideways . . . do away with the slab sides . . . make a more rounded back end. The end result was an amazing, aesthetically stunning car with sensual curves.

Victress S1A bodies were used at Bonneville in 1953, displayed and sold at the Petersen Motorama in 1952, and available thru 1965 when the Victress company was purchased by Les Dawes' company—LaDawri. Eric Hauser, Bob Powell, and other racing luminaries of the day raced cars with these bodies.

Geoff conducted comprehensive research on the Victress, collecting literature, magazine ads, and brochures and conducting interviews with people employed at the company in the early 1950s. As he gathered this material he noticed that the car in the 1955 Victress brochure had two hood scoops and that the car was in a showroom.

Geoff did not make the connection at first to the Northwest Victress with two hood scoops that he had heard about. Instead, he thought it was confusing that the Victress was in a showroom. There were no Victress showrooms.

122

Guy Dirkin bought this basket-case Victress from a collector in Oregon. Research that his friend Geoff Hacker conducted proved that this car once sat in the Petersen Publishing offices in Los Angeles. The car had been constructed by *Motor Trend*'s technical editor Fred Bodley. *Guy Dirkin*

Fastforward to 2009: One of Doc Hacker's good friends sent him a posting from a person named Terry who was selling a Victress to the highest bidder out in Oregon. Geoff had recently bought another Victress, but felt, as a researcher, compelled to get in touch with Terry and at least keep track of the car once sold. When he first talked to Terry, the car had been sold. But the would-be owner had not completed the sale. This was the second time the car had been "sold," but the deal failed to close.

Geoff kept thinking about the car in the pictures in the showroom and the connection with the car in Oregon. How many Victress cars had two hood scoops? This car had to be special . . . but how special could it be? With only 50 or fewer Victress bodies and cars estimated to have survived, Geoff felt a need to try to help find a home for the Victress, preserving the marque.

Dr. Hacker tried shopping the car to several more friends, but no one bit. Eventually, he shared the story of the Victress in Oregon with me. I have several fiberglass cars, including the 1956 Byers SR-100, a 1959 Kellison J5R, and a 1970 wide-body TVR Tuscan. I had recently bought a tube frame American Challenge/GT 1 car that I was busily pouring money into and was not particularly interested in a Victress reject located 2,000 miles away.

I did like the lines of the Victress, though, so I put up with Geoff's rantings about how I needed this car. Eventually, I called Terry and started to discuss a deal. I rationalized that I had just sold a Devin body and the cash from that deal could justify the Victress purchase.

Victress designers sought to create a sports car that "out-Jaguared" Jaguar. The styling is beautiful and mature and not typical of what one imagines as a kit car. *Guy Dirkin*

Meanwhile, Geoff's friend Tony St. Clair sent an interesting ad describing a Victress being sold in *Motor Trend* in 1955 by a guy named Don Fell at an address that looked familiar. With a bit more research, the address turned out to be Petersen Publishing Company, and when he finally located a picture of the building at that address . . . it had slanted windows. In the pictures of the Victress in the brochure, the windows in the showroom also had an unusual slant to them. Could it be that the Victress with the two hood scoops had been photographed in the Peterson Publishing Company building showroom?

Dr. Hacker was on a mission to prove or disprove that the Oregon Victress was the car in the Peterson Publishing showroom. The photograph in question was taken more than 50 years ago, and most everyone who knew about it had passed away by now. Geoff pulled out all the stops and started making phone calls to every historian he knew in California. His first successful contact was Bill Pollack, the West Coast racing legend and friend of Petersen Publishing for more than 50 years. Bill confirmed the basic layout of the building and gave Geoff more pictures of what the building looked like inside. He had no information about the Victress or its story.

Following leads, he eventually was led to Bob D'Olivio. Bob worked for Petersen back in the early 1950s and might have some knowledge that could help.

In 1960 the Alfa Romeo factory sent Lou Comito of Northport, New York two SZ coupes for entry in the 1961 Sebring 12 Hours race. Here they are in the paddock of Bridgehampton Race Circuit on Long Island. The white Alfa, now owned by Jim and Sandra McNeil, was found in a chicken coupe in 2000. *McNeil Family Collection*

Geoff called Bob D'Olivio and introduced himself as a car historian and researcher. He asked Bob about Petersen Publishing Company and if they displayed cars in the office, and he said . . . yes, for a few years through the mid-1950s. Later, they expanded the offices inside and there was no longer room. But early on . . . there was.

Great! Did Bob remember a car being built by Fred Bodley? Geoff asked this question because the ad showing the Victress for sale by Don Fell stated that the car was originally built by the late technical editor for *Motor Trend*, Fred Bodley. Geoff waited in anticipation for Bob to answer: Yes, he did; it was white and was a Victress. Dr. Hacker took this testimonial as proof the Victress in question had been shown in the Peterson Publishing Company showroom.

Fred Bodley was technical editor for *Motor Trend* magazine from January 1952 until his death in 1955. The Victress was built for street use and race events, and as the advertisement pointed out, the car managed to accumulate only 80 miles before Bodley died.

Geoff called to tell me about the rapidly uncovered history. Before he could dazzle me with his newfound information, I enthusiastically jump-started the conversation. "Hi, Geoff, funny you should call. I just put the phone down with Terry. We just cut a deal, and I am shipping the Victress to Chicago next week if everything works out."

The project Victress (left) has a beautiful garage companion at the Dirkin house, his restored Byers SR-100. *Guy Dirkin*

"You bought the car?" he asked. "Well, let me tell you what you just bought." Geoff started to recount the details of his findings. Pretty cool stuff.

So many early specials have scant history. This Victress S1A was built by a guy who had the expertise to do a good job (Bodley ran a Rolls-Royce repair shop) and was tied into the emerging Peterson Publishing Company with *Motor Trend* magazine. In the early 1950s, *Motor Trend* was not a product buried deep in a large corporate publishing empire. The guys writing and pulling the magazine together were enthusiasts writing for enthusiasts. Fred Bodley was part of a small team—not quite three men and a dog, but close. Certainly, projects like the Victress were the grist for *Motor Trend* at the time. The staff was engaged in their projects and wrote about them.

At the time of writing, I am moving forward with restoring the car, and I look forward to the car's debut, at a future Amelia Island Concours d'Elegance event perhaps.

The hunt for old cars is a fun and enjoyable part of the hobby, for sure. In the case of the Victress, others before me had turned down the option to own a sorry-looking Northwestern weathered basket case. With the help of Dr. Geoff Hacker's research, things turned out to be way more interesting. Restoring the car runs in parallel with the preservation of a story that can be passed on. I find I am drawn to cars with something more to offer than a low VIN number or an unusual set of factory options. The Victress S1A and other specials allow one to be associated with the past passion of the builders. Passion endures.

A Healey in the Shadows

Women have tried to convince men to clear out and sell their extra things since the dawn of civilization. While the story of a wife convincing her aging husband to sell his cars is a barn-find cliché, Porsche enthusiast John Helgesen knows that those stories can have positive results.

In 2004, Helgesen got a call from his sister, a professor at Agnes Scott College near Atlanta, asking a favor on behalf of the wife of fellow professor, Seaborn Jones. "My sister had been friends with the Jones family for ages," said Helgesen. "The professor's wife, Penny, was trying to convince her husband to sell the two old cars in the garage and asked if I would help determine their value."

He knew one of the cars was a 1963 Porsche 356B; the other was some sort of British car. The cars had been sitting for at least 29 years, their mechanical condition unknown.

Helgesen lived four hours away in South Carolina, so he posted photos his sister emailed to him of the Porsche on the Pelican Parts website and asked viewers to give estimates of the car's value. The estimates ranged from $8,000 to $30,000.

One of the folks who viewed the website was Steve Drabant, 34, of Atlanta. Even though Drabant was also a Porsche enthusiast, he was more interested in the "British" car in the background. He was told by Helgesen that it was some sort of Healey, but those conversations quickly came to an end when Professor Jones decided he didn't want to sell the cars anyway.

Helgesen stayed in touch with the Jones family and, in 2007, received a phone call that Seaborn had passed away.

"They asked my sister to be the executor of the estate, and she asked if I could help out," he said. "But I was a 911 guy, not a 356 guy. I thought it would be easier to manage if the car was at my house rather than four hours away. But my sister wanted the car to stay there for Seaborn's memorial service; she wanted everyone to walk by the car on the way into the house. Sometime after Thanksgiving, I drove down with my F-250 pickup and trailer to pick it up."

When he arrived at the Jones house, he found the Porsche had been parked since 1971 and had 57,000 miles on the odometer. Jones had purchased the one-year-old car from the original owner in 1964.

One of the wheels was frozen and had to be broken loose, and Helgesen noted a petrified rat under the car. After a few hours of work, the Porsche

John Helgesen was asked to help the family of a professor by selling their Porsche. Helgesen was drawn to the 356 himself, but his friend Steve Drabant saw something up-front that interested him more, "Some sort of British car in the background." *John Helgesen*

was sitting in front of Helgesen's home. "But it sat in my box trailer for at least two months while I was finishing up a new garage," he said. "During our New Year's Eve party, we unveiled the Porsche."

Helgesen began to check over the car and discovered that it was in pretty good shape with very solid floorpans. "It was a 356B S-model, which had seventy-five horsepower," said Helgesen.

Then Helgesen's wife, Tonya, sat in the driver's seat, the first person to do so in 36 years. "She said it was cute," he said.

The couple decided to try to purchase the Porsche and began to negotiate with Penny Jones. "This would be an opportunity to have a car we normally wouldn't own," he said.

Ultimately they were successful and purchased the car. They invited all their Porsche friends over for a bratwurst party to celebrate their new purchase.

"I've decided to leave it as-is, because I might get lynched by the 356 community if I try to restore it," he said. "It only has a few rock chips on the nose, but other than that, it is as solid as could be.

"I'm a little bit afraid to drive it on roads with all those soccer moms driving those big SUVs. I almost got wiped out just driving to Dunkin Donuts one Saturday morning.

"I don't want anything to happen to this car, because it means too much to me."

That's the story of the Porsche. But remember the other car in Jones' garage, the British some-kind-of-Healey?

Well, Steve Drabant of Atlanta stayed in touch with Helgesen, and when Penny Jones decided to sell the car, he jumped on it.

"I saw this car in the background," said Drabant. "Everyone wanted to know what it was. It turned out being a 1957 Austin Healey 100-6, a very early Longbridge car. Well, I've always wanted a big Healey."

Drabant was a little bit short on cash at the moment, but he turned his father onto the car. Steve caught the British car bug from his dad, who also owns a couple of vintage MGBs.

After a 30-year hibernation, the little Porsche cleaned up pretty well. The car is a 356B and had only 57,000 miles on the odometer. After he cleaned out the petrified rat from under the car and loosened a stuck brake, he decided to drive the car as-is. *Bob Chapman/Excellence magazine*

Further investigation revealed the car was a 2+2, was Primrose Yellow with a black hardtop, and had only 49,000 miles on the odometer.

"Seaborn Jones was actually the original owner of the car," said Drabant. "The best anyone could figure out, the car had been parked in that garage for forty years. It was originally purchased in Utah, then moved to Florida, and finally Georgia, all dry states, which is why the body survived in such good shape."

A deal was struck for $3,500, which Steve is more than pleased with. "It was an incredible deal," he said. "I'm so lucky that it was posted on a Porsche website, because there weren't many potential purchasers for it there."

Once he got the car home in December 2008, Drabant went through all the brake lines, fuel lines, fuel pump, and electrical system, and he installed new ignition points and had the gas tank dipped. But when he went to fire it up, there was no spark.

"It turned out that one of the insulators on the points was backwards, so it was shorting out," he said. "Once I got that sorted, it fired right up."

For Drabant, the most fun was digging through the trunk and glove box and discovering the previous owner's mementos. He found several TSD Rally plaques, an SCCA grille badge, and literature from a 1960 Savannah road race.

Drabant, also a Porsche enthusiast, fell in love with the Healey parked in front of the Porsche. It's a 1957 100-6 that was a one-owner 49,000-mile car. Steve is presently refurbishing the Healey for his dad. *Steve Drabant*

Additionally, the car had Marchal headlights and driving lights, so Drabant suspects it was used in road rallies in the late 1950s and 1960s.

"Ultimately my dad will take possession of the Healey, but I'm just glad I was able to find it for him and work on it a little bit," he said.

The Luckiest Guy
in the Room

Donnie Gould is probably the luckiest guy in the room, one of those guys who always seem to be in the right place at the right time. You know, the kind of guy who had the best-looking girlfriend in high school, and every coin he finds on the ground is always facing heads-up.

But as a wise man once said, you make your own luck, and Gould certainly has made his own. Gould is a partner in the RM Auction organization, which puts on world-class events in Monterey, Amelia Island, and around the world. So he is constantly in tune with cars and collections that have potential as auction candidates.

Prior to joining RM, the 48-year-old man owned Donnie Gould Restorations in Vero Beach, Florida. His shop was known for authentic restorations performed for some of the hobby's biggest players. For instance, he was charged with restoring Donald Campbell's *Bluebird* for NASCAR's France family. This priceless speed-record car is proudly displayed today in the lobby of Daytona USA.

Below are a couple of Gould's more intriguing finds:

The Cobra in the Closet

"A kid called the RM office in Michigan one night and said he had a Cobra to sell," said Gould, who lives in Fort Lauderdale.

"The guys in the office thought it was a prank call, but called me to check out the serial numbers in the Cobra Register. I mean, what kid owns a Cobra? In the register I read that the car was last known to be in the Salt Lake City, Utah, area, which is where the kid was calling from."

When photos came across Gould's computer screen the next morning, he was on a flight from Fort Lauderdale to Salt Lake City on a car-hunting expedition.

"We had already negotiated a price with the kid on the phone, so I had cash in my pocket," he said. "Because if it was a for-real car, I needed to close the deal right away before word got out," he said.

The kid turned out to be the young nephew of the Cobra's owner. It seems that his uncle offered a deal to his young relative; if he could sell the Cobra for more than $X amount, he could keep the balance. That was enough to put the kid's entrepreneurial mind in gear.

The longtime owners of 289 Cobra, CSX2171, kept it hidden inside a secret closet in their Salt Lake City garage because they were tired of neighbors inquiring about the car every time the garage door was open. Here, Mrs. Christiansen reveals the secret hideaway where the Cobra languished for nearly 40 years. *Donnie Gould*

He had previously called a well-known Salt Lake City Cobra collector, the late Larry Miller, to see if he was interested in buying the car, but the call was never returned, so he called RM.

The Shelby Register said the car had two known owners, and the last owner purchased it in 1967 for $3,500. It came from Shelby American with a hard top and a luggage rack.

When Gould arrived at the house, the garage door was open, but no Cobra was to be seen. He met the owner, the uncle of the kid who called, and he explained that he became tired of people inquiring about the Cobra every time his garage door was open. So he built a hidden closet inside his garage, just big enough for a Cobra to fit.

"He actually built a set of Dutch doors that closed behind the Cobra with curtains above so the car was completely hidden from view if the garage door was open," Gould said.

Stored above the Cobra, though, was something that gave Gould chills.

"He had a Model A Ford pickup cab tied above the Cobra with a piece of rope," said Gould. "I asked him what he would do if the rope broke, but he didn't seem worried. Fortunately that never happened."

The Cobra had an early 1970s inspection sticker on the windshield and

Saying goodbye to the former closet-queen, the Christiansens helped purchaser Donnie Gould push the Cobra out into the daylight for the first time since Richard Nixon was in the White House. *Donnie Gould*

49,000 miles on the odometer. Gould was curious why the man was selling such a nice unrestored car.

"He was a retired doctor, and he and his wife were opening a picture frame outlet," said Gould. "He needed to invest in his new business, but said the Cobra was the best investment he had ever made."

When Gould said he would buy the car at the agreed-upon price, he was surprised to discover that the price had magically gone up overnight.

"They tried to beat me up for another twenty thousand dollars," he said, "but I managed to convince them that a deal was a deal."

Gould had the car picked up and transported to his shop in Florida, where he did a thorough mechanical appraisal of the new purchase. He was extremely pleased with what he found.

"After forty years, we dumped some gas in the tank and it fired right up!" said Gould. "We rebuilt the brakes and cleaned up the calipers, installed a new clutch and re-gasketed the engine. The car still had its original fan belt!

"We made it one hundred percent reliable, so you could drive it fast anywhere."

Gould arranged for his friend Jim Taylor to purchase the car from RM. Taylor is a renowned collector from New York who was seeking a unique 289 Cobra to use on classic car tours.

"It's running great," said Taylor. "Donnie spent several months fiddling with it, and it's running like a top. I'm not afraid of getting wet, which is good because I can't fit in the car with the top in place anyway.

"We're going to leave it all original, the dirt and everything. We haven't washed it yet.

"Everyone who knows anything about Cobras goes bananas over that car."

Daytona Crash-O-Rama Mercury

When Donnie Gould was growing up, his father was friends with Big Bill France, founder of NASCAR and Daytona International Speedway. So lucky little Donnie would get full pit and garage credentials for the Daytona 500 when he was a kid.

The impressions of speed and mechanics he'd witness at these races would leave an impression on him into adulthood.

One of those impressions was of the 1976 Daytona 500 when the blue No. 43 Plymouth of Richard Petty was racing door-handle-to-door-handle with the red and white No. 21 Mercury of David Pearson.

To quote Greg Fielden from his great *Forty Years of Stock Car Racing* series of books:

Petty took the lead with 13 laps to go. Pearson tucked inside Petty's slipstream and followed his rival until the backstretch on the last lap. Pearson pulled out of the draft and passed Petty for the lead. Pearson then drifted up high in the third turn, opening the door for Petty and setting the stage for the final lap fireworks.

Petty's car broke loose slightly as they came off the fourth turn side-by-side. Pearson bobbled as Petty took a one car-length advantage onto the short chute. But suddenly, both cars started spinning and crashing into the wall.

Pearson's car twirled and hit Joe Frasson's Chevrolet at the entrance to pit road. Through all the excitement, Pearson had the presence of mind to engage the clutch—and therefore kept his motor running.

Petty fishtailed down the track before darting up into the wall. His car spun around and came to a halt in the infield 100 feet short of the finish line. His engine was dead.

Pearson knocked his car into gear and crossed under Harold Kinder's checkered flag at no more than 20 mph.

Petty's crew ran from the pits and pushed their driver across the finish line.

Hidden behind his other automotive projects, Gould discovered the famous David Pearson/Wood Brothers Mercury in a Florida junkyard. The car had languished in two junkyards after serving as a Winston Brand show car for many years. But Gould's detective skills identified it as one of the most desirable NASCAR stock cars. *Donnie Gould*

It was a crash-fest to the finish, with Pearson limping across the line to win, Petty coming in second.

So when Gould saw an old Mercury stock car in a Vero Beach, Florida, junkyard, his memory of that race came rushing back.

"I was searching junkyards for a set of Bui3ck finned aluminum brake drums for a Miller IndyCar I was restoring," said Gould. "I didn't find the brake drums I needed, but my buddy called me over to look at a car under a lean-to. It was an old Mercury stock car.

"I said to my friend, 'What is this thing?' but when I looked under the hood and saw the Holman-Moody-style chassis, there was no doubt that this was a real stock car."

Gould approached the junkyard owner and asked about the car under the lean-to.

"Aw, you can't afford that car," is all the man said.

After the 1976 Daytona race, Pearson's Mercury was repaired at the Wood Brothers' Shop in Stuart, Virginia, and he continued to race it to one of the most successful NASCAR seasons ever, with 10 wins and 7 poles.

After the 1981 season, though, NASCAR legislated new shorter-wheelbase cars, so older cars like the Mercury Cyclone became obsolete.

The car could still be used as a promotional vehicle, however, so it was sold to R.J. Reynolds Tobacco for conversion into a show car. It was painted bright red and white, with "Winston #1" emblazoned on the sides, and was shown at trade shows and consumer events around the country for several years.

When the Mercury's days as a show car were over in the early 1980s, the car was purchased from R.J. Reynolds by struggling race driver Richard Childress (who became a successful team owner). Childress stripped off all the good parts for use on his own race car, then gave the chassis back to the Wood Brothers. It sat behind their Stuart, Virginia, shop for years.

One day a local Stuart area junkyard owner purchased the chassis for $200 and hauled it off to his yard. The Wood Brothers thought it was the last anyone would see of that car once the man's cutting torches dissected the chassis.

Rather than cut up the carcass, the man put it under a lean-to next to some old school buses.

Eventually the junkyard owner decided he needed to live in a nicer climate, so he bought some land in Vero Beach, Florida, and moved the entire contents of his junkyard south to Florida.

So one day this young guy (Gould) comes into the Vero Beach junkyard asking for some finned aluminum brake drums and stumbles across the old stocker under the lean-to. After the owner told him he couldn't afford the car, Gould went home and did his homework.

He called the Wood Brothers and asked them for information about the Daytona 500–winning Mercury.

"They said it had been sold to a junker in Stuart, but the yard had been moved to Florida," said Gould. "Bingo!"

Gould went back to the Vero Beach junkyard owner and asked how much he wanted for the Mercury.

"He said if I pay him what he had in it—one thousand two hundred dollars—I could own this Daytona 500–winning chassis," said Gould. "So the old guy knew what he had.

"I paid him the one thousand two hundred dollars and hauled it back to my shop, where it sat for three or four years, because I didn't have the money to work on it," he said.

"It had a Banjo Matthews chassis, one of the first he built. Banjo bought the chassis jigs from Holman-Moody when they had their big auction, and he built his chassis the same way."

Gould called the Wood Brothers shop and started to ask them questions about the car. They were eager to help, but suggested he take lots of photos of the car and bring them up to their shop. It was a long trip from South Florida to Stuart, Virginia, but Gould gladly jumped in his truck and drove north.

"I felt bad, because the team was getting ready to go to Daytona—they were really busy—but they all spent time with me," said Gould. "And they went into their store rooms and gave me some significant parts they still had for that car—stainless-steel headers, a Ford 351-cubic-inch block, heads, and a brand-new wiring harness."

Once Gould collected all the parts necessary to restore the Mercury, he devoted most of his time to the project. "I worked on the car for three months full-time, and when I started to run out of money, I started to take on some customer work for another three months," he said.

"But once I had it finished, I didn't know what to do with it. I displayed it at Daytona and took some parade laps before the 1995 Daytona 500, but man, what else could I do with it?"

This Mercury was one of the first NASCAR stockers to have disc brakes. Actually, Gould sourced the brakes as a monster set of Hurst-Airheart disc brakes originally manufactured for a motor home.

Gould competed in several vintage races with the Mercury, but because the car was so authentic, he said he wasn't very competitive against some of the more modified vintage stock cars running today.

"All those other cars have been lightened and have modern engines, so I couldn't compete with the other guys," he said. "And it handled poorly on the road courses."

Eventually Gould sold the Mercury to "Speedy" Bill Smith, owner of Speedway Motors in Lincoln, Nebraska. The car sits in Speedy's museum.

Does Gould miss owning the car?

"I've owned hundreds and hundreds of cars in my life, and it's the only one that I regret selling," he said.

Gould tells a final quick story about a special appearance he once was invited to.

"In 1998, I was invited to display the Mercury at the Purolator Party the night before the Daytona 500," he said. "The Wood Brothers team was there, and they walked around and around the car. It's like they didn't want to leave it.

"Then here comes Richard Petty to look at the car. He looks at the car and walks around it, checking out the restoration. Then he just kicks the tire.

"I hate this car," he said as he walked away.

The American Motors Mercury

Owners of collector cars are often the first to hear about other desirable cars. When I owned a Morris Minor, people came out of the woodwork to tell me about other Morris Minors they knew about, so I know this phenomenon firsthand.

Donnie Gould knows this too.

Gould heard about another Mercury stock car in Connecticut. He dragged it home to Florida and quickly realized that this car didn't start out its racing life as a Merc. Instead, it began as a Penske AMC Matador that had been driven by Bobby Allison, then was a Mercury driven by Ricky Rudd, Dave Marcis, and Bill Elliott. *Donnie Gould*

Because of the publicity his beautifully restored 1976 Mercury garnered, he heard about other old stock cars hiding in barns. One of those stories got his attention.

"Fifteen years ago, I got a call from a guy who lived in Connecticut," said Gould. "He told me he had this old Mercury NASCAR stock car lying in a pasture that he wanted to sell."

Gould jumped in his truck and made the long road trip to the Constitution State, more than a 24-hour drive away. He purchased the car for $5,000, but once he got it home, he discovered it was probably not the car it appeared to be.

"It's the old Penske Racing Cam 2–sponsored car," he said. "And I think it started life as an AMC Matador, not a Mercury."

Gould said that many of the mechanical pieces under the hood had been nickel-plated for aesthetic purposes. Gould said that Penske would hire a designer to advise him about where to place colors and finishes on his cars.

"To make his cars more aesthetically pleasing, he'd have a designer tell him what to paint and what to plate to make his cars look pretty," said Gould.

Gould's research ultimately concluded that this car is the one remaining Matador, because the other one was destroyed in a Bristol wreck. After

Gould has documents from Penske Racing that indicate his Mercury's chassis once started life as a Matador, possibly this one, shown under construction in the Penske shop in 1976. *Donnie Gould collection*

sandblasting the car, he found some American Motors chassis numbers near the rear of the frame, specifically K20 AM and K28 D6.

"This is the car, that Bobby Allison drove for Penske in 1976 before it was rebodied and raced as a Mercury by Dave Marcis in 1977," he said. "In 1978, the car was sold to George Elliott, Bill Elliott's father, and was driven by Bill in 1979.

"The car was then sold to Junie Dunlavey and was raced by Ricky Rudd."

Gould explains that this is the car on which Penske mounted the massive brakes from a Porsche 917 when it was campaigned for Allison in 1976.

Gould will restore the car as a Penske Matador, but for the time being, the car is coated in epoxy primer and sitting in his Florida shop waiting for some free time to open up in the busy man's schedule.

The Dynamic Duo

Jeff Trask is one of those lucky guys who has a barn-finding buddy, someone he wouldn't leave for a barn-finding expedition without. His friend is Pete McNulty, and according to Trask, he is the automotive equivalent of Crocodile Dundee.

"He's the kind of guy who shows up in coveralls with a winch, tools, and all the know-how to excavate cars," says Trask, 50, from Santa Ana, California. "He's a resourceful Irishman, a jack-of-all-trades who can get a car that hasn't moved in thirty years up on a trailer.

"There is no better guy to take along."

Trask and McNulty have been searching for and buying cars together for decades. Trask figures they have purchased more than 100 cars together—mostly Porsches—since they first met.

Until recently, Trask sold and brokered yachts in Newport Beach, California. Since selling his successful dealership, he has become a full-time automotive archeologist. McNulty sells commercial floor cleaning equipment during the week. But on weekends, the two are usually in a Ford F-250 pickup, towing a trailer and driving up and down the West Coast in search of vintage tin.

The agreement they have is this: it doesn't matter who finds the car, it belongs to both of them. When they sell it, the profits are split 50-50, less repair costs.

Trask managed to slow down long enough to tell me a few of their more memorable barn-finding tales. He reminds us, though, that he doesn't fall head over heels for the cars he finds. "I can't afford to," he said. "This is how I make my living now. I'm a flipper. For me it's all about the find, not the romance."

Porsche's Holy Grail

"My wife and I were out looking for real estate for a second home," said Trask. "We were looking in the California Central Valley, between Mariposa and Grass Valley, which is about six hours from our house.

"It's called the Gold Country, because of all the gold mines that used to be in the area."

Trask never realized when he rode around with the realtor that day, he'd discover another kind of gold.

"We were with the realtor driving through an area around Murphys, Angels Camp, and Sutter Creek, all old mining towns," he said.

The longtime owner of this Porsche Speedster bought it in 1962 and parked it under this lean-to in 1979. He casually mentioned to Jeff Trask that he owned an old Porsche, and Trask bought it in 2007. *Jeff Trask*

"We had already spent a couple of days with him when he said to me, 'Your wife tells me you are into old Porsches.'"

Trask said he was, not thinking much of it, until the realtor said, "Well, I have one of those."

Trask's brain quickly changed from house-mode to Porsche-mode.

"Oh, what do you have?" he asked.

"It's an old convertible," said the realtor. "It's been parked since 1979 and I haven't driven it since. I have it parked at my farm. Would you like to see it?"

So they made plans to look at the car the next morning before they departed for home, six hours away.

"My wife wasn't into it because we had a long drive ahead of us," said Trask. "But we met him on the corner in the small town of Galt, where he asked us to.

"We drove down this long driveway about one mile away. It was totally overgrown, and we drove through two-foot-high grass. But when we got to the end, I could see a Porsche-shaped car that was covered with a tarp."

When they peeled away the cover, Trask realized he was looking at one of the most desirable Porsches ever built—a 1958 Speedster.

The car was as dry as a bone under a carport that was attached to a garage. He grabbed his Porsche 356 reference book, which he never leaves home without.

Jeff Trask (right), not Jerry Seinfeld, proudly takes possession of a spectacular 1966 Porsche 911 from its original owner Ken Fielding. The car had been a PCA Concours champion many times before it went into long-term storage in a bat-infested warehouse. *Pete McNulty photo*

The numbers matched up. This was an untouched, original car.

"I was hoping my son would restore it," said the realtor. "But he has never really shown any interest."

Trask learned the story of how the man acquired the Speedster. He grew up in Oregon, and after college, in 1962, he purchased the car from the original owner. He had used the car as his everyday transportation until he moved to California to pursue a career in real estate.

"He loaded everything he had into the little Porsche and drove it down to California," said Trask. "He knew the little two-seater wouldn't be very practical to haul around clients, so he parked it under the lean-to in 1979, and it has sat there until 2007, almost thirty years.

"We talked about the car, and I told him I'd be interested in buying it if he was interested in parting with it. Or, if he wanted it restored, I could recommend a shop, either way."

The man said he had to talk to his son first.

Trask made an offer on the Porsche, and as he and his wife drove down the driveway, finally on their way home, he was already on his cell phone calling friends and telling them about his find.

This 911 was the Porsche barn-find of a lifetime. The interior still looked new, and the odometer showed only 23,800 miles. Trask and McNulty purchased the car with three sets of wheels, all in concours condition. *Jeff Trask photo*

"I called Pete and three or four other guys," he said. "I was getting that giddy feeling I get every time I find an interesting car.

"Pete said, 'Whatever you need, I'll help you.'"

A few days later the phone rang; it was the realtor. He said he had spoken to his son, who had no real interest in owning his father's old Porsche. So Trask's offer was accepted.

"I know the right people to buy vintage Porsches, so I had the car sold before I ever got there to pick it up," he said.

"All I can say is that the McNulty and Trask families enjoyed a nice windfall profit that day.

"I'd say in the world of hunting for Porsche 356s, the Speedster and the 550 Spider are the two Holy Grails. I've found one, now I'm looking for the other."

Bat Guano Porsche

Friends McNulty and Trask were on their way to purchase another Porsche, this time a 912 Targa. Trask said that counter to the opinions of many enthusiasts, his favorite Porsche is the four-cylinder 912.

"I find they have the best balance of any Porsche I've driven," said Trask.

So the two pals were in the Ford F-250 pickup truck en route to purchase a 1967 Porsche 912 Targa, a fairly rare model with only 550 built.

"We were on our way up to Woodland, California, to look at the 912," he said. "If we bought it, we'd rent a U-Haul trailer to drag it home. It didn't make much sense to drag a trailer all the way up there."

As they drove, passing through Santa Barbara, they noticed a Porsche repair shop off the side of the road. Through experience, they knew they had to stop.

They walked in and asked the proprietor if he knew of any old Porsches for sale in the area.

"Well, there is this one 911 in the back that belongs to our building landlord," said the man, who didn't know if it was actually for sale. "Would you like to see it?" he asked as he guided Trask and McNulty into the back of the cavernous building.

They walked through a door that the mechanic opened with a key. It revealed a large, old wooden room with high ceilings and a motor home parked across the room. The three had to shimmy between the motor home's bumper and the wall to get to the other side, where they saw a Porsche-sized car covered with a tarp.

"It was covered with a plastic tarp, but it was obvious that it was up in the air on jack stands," said Trask.

"Would you like to see it?" asked the man.

"Yes, but what is all that white stuff all over the tarp," asked Trask. "And what is that smell?"

"Oh, that's bat shit," he said.

Bats inhabited the upper rafters of the building and had used the car for target practice for many, many years.

The man shimmied his way past the motor home again and retrieved work gloves from his shop. He handed them to McNulty and Trask, and they began to peel away the dreck-covered plastic cover.

Then they peeled off another cover and another. The car had at least four fitted cloth covers on it before they could see paint. But then, oh, my . . . .

"I started to get that giddy feeling again," said Trask. "This car had perfect red paint. It was a California black-plate car and was currently registered, even though it hadn't been out of the garage in many years.

"The owner peeled up the covers of the car to stick on a new registration sticker each year. We call that a 'stack-of-stickers in California.'"

The Porsche mechanic gave Trask and McNulty the owner's phone number. His name was Ken Fielding, and Trask immediately left a message on his answering machine.

The two were on their way home, McNulty driving the Ford truck and Trask driving their newly purchased Porsche 912, which turned out to be a solid, good-running car. Halfway home, Trask's cell phone rang.

"Is this Jeff?" asked the man. "This is Ken Fielding, and I own the Porsche you were looking at."

Trask learned that the man was 83 years old and had purchased the 911 brand-new in 1966. He participated for many years in Porsche Club of America Porsche Parade Concours events, where his car often took home the gold.

The 911 had been parked in the building he owned in 1975, immediately following that year's Porsche Parade Concours, where he won first place.

"He said he had always wanted to work on it, but hadn't gotten the time lately," said Trask. "I could tell he was kind of old, probably bordering on senility because he repeated himself and rambled so often.

"I told him I was interested in the car, and he asked what I would offer.

"I told him I was no Jerry Seinfeld," and he got a good chuckle out of that. The comedian and Porsche collector has a reputation for paying very high amounts of money for original old Porsches.

Kept under multiple car covers in a bat-infested warehouse for decades, this nearly perfect low-mileage 1966 911 Porsche thankfully survived unscathed. Trask and his friend Pete McNulty were able to purchase the 23,800-mile car from the original owner in July 2009. *Jeff Trask*

Fielding had an idea of what the car was worth. Trask made him an offer and was told he'd hear from him in a few days.

"My son-in-law has always been interested in the car, so I need to call him first," Fielding said before he hung up.

"I knew I'd probably never hear from him again, so I just forgot about it," said Trask. "I didn't hear from him for a couple of months, and then one day as my wife and I were driving to Monterey for the historic races, my cell phone rang."

"I've been thinking about this," said Fielding. "My son-in-law doesn't really appreciate the Porsche, and you do."

Fielding told Trask how much money he wanted for the car and Trask agreed.

"He told me he was going to get his extra parts together and call me in a week, when I returned from Monterey," said Trask.

"So I was at the bank pulling out the funds to buy the car when my cell phone rang."

"Hello, Jeff," said Fielding. "This is Ken. Say, I've been thinking about the Porsche and I've decided that I'm going to restore the Porsche myself. Besides, Mike [the mechanic at the Porsche shop] told me he could get me more money for the car than you had offered.

"I just need more money, but if you're willing to pay. . . ."

Trask reminded Fielding of something he said during their first conversation.

"Remember, Ken, I'm no Jerry Seinfeld," he said.

The phone call ended with neither party feeling satisfied. Then two weeks later, Fielding called again.

"Say, I've been feeling terrible that I didn't honor our agreement," said Fielding. "I've stopped the sale to the other gentleman. I'm an honorable man and I'm going to sell the car to you."

Trask wasn't taking any chances; the next day he was at Fielding's door with cash in his hand. On July 14, 2009, Trask and McNulty finally picked up the 911.

True to his word, Fielding assembled the extra parts, including three sets of wheels and tires (one set of standard steel wheels, a rare set of Fuchs alloy rims, and a set of chrome rims). He also handed Trask the four brake calipers, which had been drained and individually wrapped up at the time of its long-term hibernation. At the same time, Fielding flushed, drained, and capped the brake lines.

"The car is like new," said Trask. "It has only twenty-three thousand eight hundred miles on it since new. The paint looks like it just came out of the showroom."

The Closing Door

It was a Saturday and Trask had just finished helping a friend move a refrigerator with his pickup truck and was on his way home.

"I was driving through this neighborhood, and I was doing what I usually do—looking left and right as I rode down the road," he said.

To the left something caught his attention; it was definitely a green sports car, possibly a Sunbeam. And there was a second car, but the garage door was already one-third down, and within another second, it was closed.

"I said to myself, 'Oh, boy, maybe it's a Sunbeam Tiger,'" as he began to turn around and go back to the house.

"I knocked on the door and a little old lady answered. I asked if that was a Sunbeam I saw, and she said yes."

"That was my husband's," she said. "He bought it brand-new in 1967. But he is in a nursing home now because he needs full-time care."

Trask asked if he could take a look at the car, and she agreed. She opened the garage door and Trask feasted his eyes on two relics.

"On the left side was a British Racing Green Sunbeam Alpine, not a Tiger," he said. "On the right side was an Aston Martin DB2-4 MK III. I could tell the Aston was all there."

The Aston was on jack stands, and the Alpine had a thick layer of dust on it.

Trask was getting that giddy feeling again.

The woman told him that her husband had purchased the Aston Martin in 1971 and it had been in the garage since 1980. It leaked oil from the pan gasket, and her husband had not found the time to replace it.

"Would you sell them to me?" he asked the woman.

"Well, I'm selling the house to pay for his medical bills and moving into a trailer," she said. "Yes, I'd consider selling them. But you'll need to talk to my daughter about them, because she handles my finances."

Trask did some research and called the daughter with his offer. She in turn made a few phone calls and even had a friend who was a car enthusiast come over to inspect the cars.

Trask's offer was accepted.

"I made a fair offer and they got a fair deal," he said. "All parties made out on the deal."

Put your hand over the top half of this photo, and that's all that Jeff Trask saw as the garage door was closing when he drove past. He could identify a Sunbeam, hoping it was a Tiger, but couldn't identify the other car, which turned out to be an Aston-Martin DB2-4. *Jeff Trask*

The elderly owner, who was in a nursing home, purchased this Sunbeam Alpine new in 1967. The man's wife was forced to sell his prized possessions to offset high medical expenses. *Jeff Trask*

This Aston-Martin was purchased by the man in 1971 and parked in 1980 with a leaky oil pan gasket. Within hours of buying the two cars, Trask had both of them repaired and running like new. *Jeff Trask*

An arrangement was made to retrieve his purchases. He said the most fascinating part about picking up the cars was taking the Aston Martin off the jack stands.

"The car has an aluminum body with skinny rails and chassis members," he said, not wanting to make a mistake and raise it at a vulnerable location. "I had a two-ton jack and rolled it to a crossmember directly behind the transmission mount."

As he raised the jack, the weight came off all four jack stands at once. He was able to slide all four jack stands from beneath the car at the same time.

"I found it amazing that the car was so perfectly balanced from that one location on the chassis," said Trask. He lowered the car gently to the ground.

The Aston Martin's four tires needed air, but the Sunbeam's tires were still inflated.

"Both cars rolled easily, and thankfully no brakes were stuck," he said.

Both cars were loaded on transporters by noon that Saturday morning and brought back to his shop. The oil was changed in both cars, plugs cleaned, and batteries charged, and by 4 p.m., both cars were purring away.

"Both cars ran like sewing machines," he said.

The Father & Son Hunting Team

Don and Keith Isley have the perfect father-and-son hobby: searching for old cars. The two have developed an eye for seeing cars that are virtually invisible to most enthusiasts.

Take the Corvette that appears on the cover of this book. It was discovered by son Keith as the family was driving home to Greensboro, North Carolina, from a vacation in Myrtle Beach, South Carolina, four or five years ago.

"We had been driving for four or five hours," said Keith, 17. That's when he said to his father, "Stop!"

Father Don thought something was the matter, so he quickly came to a stop.

"What's the matter?" he asked his son.

"There's a 1970 Dodge Challenger back there."

So, as they had done so many times before, Don turned around the family car and drove back to the Challenger on the side of the road. All this happened without waking up a sleeping Mrs. Isley in the back seat.

The two enthusiasts spoke to the car's owner for 30 to 40 minutes. The car wasn't for sale, so they kept driving up the road.

One mile later, Keith yelled, "Stop!"

"Now what?" asked Don.

"I saw something in an old garage," answered Keith. "I think it might have been James Dean's Porsche." Keith, at the time 12 years old, certainly had a robust imagination.

"No more stopping, we need to get home," said Don, who had more than an hour left to drive before they pulled in their driveway. Mrs. Isley still hadn't woken from her sleep.

Keith never forgot that car in the garage. It was more than 100 feet off the road, surrounded by trees and partially blocked from view by cardboard boxes and other trash.

Six months later, again returning from a weekend at Myrtle Beach, he remembered the garage and this time convinced his dad to stop.

Instead of James Dean's Porsche 550 Spyder, the car-hunting duo found an old Corvette parked in the open garage. It was the ideal barn find.

"We knocked on the door of the house, but nobody was home," said Don, 48. "So I left a business card in his mailbox with a note and kept driving toward home."

See the hidden sports car in the garage? This is the view eagle-eyed barn-finder Keith Isley saw on the way home from a family vacation. From the little bit he saw, he thought it might be the remains of James Dean's Porsche 550 Spider. When they drove up the driveway, they discovered it was "only" a Corvette. *Tom Cotter*

The Isleys never heard from the Corvette's owner, so Don did an Internet search for the name on the mailbox. Calling the phone number, he spoke to the woman who answered.

"Oh, that car belongs to my son," she said. "His number is unlisted, but I'll give it to you."

The next phone call began a relationship that continues today, nearly six years later.

The car belonged to Bill McKinnon, who purchased the 1960 Corvette as a used car in 1967 for $1,200. "I was nineteen or twenty years old and found it on a used car lot in Asheboro [North Carolina]. There were two Corvettes on the lot, a customized one and this one, which was original. I decided the original one looked better, so I bought it. The car had about sixty thousand miles on it when I bought it."

It was McKinnon's everyday car from 1967 until the mid-1980s, when he parked it in his garage with about 120,000 miles on the odometer.

"We offered to buy the car from Bill, but it wasn't for sale," said Don. "Then we offered to take the car out of his garage, clean the car and the garage, and install a proper garage door, but he said it could stay there just fine.

This is what they saw when they got up close: a 1960 Corvette that had sat since the mid-1980s. The car had clearly seen better days. *Tom Cotter*

"So I asked him if we could stop by and visit next time we drove by, and Bill said, 'Sure.'"

The Isleys also offered to bring the Corvette to a warehouse his brother owned in Greensboro for secure storage. They even offered to get the car running and go through the mechanics, but McKinnon wasn't interested.

On one of the family's biannual trips to Myrtle Beach, Don and Keith stopped at McKinnon's and gave him a gift: a copy of my book, *The Hemi in the Barn*. Inside they wrote a nice message and their name and phone number.

"Our fingers are still crossed that one day we'll get that phone call from Bill that he's ready to sell us the car," said Don.

Buying a Collector's Collection

The Isley boys, father Don and son Keith, have it figured out. Rather than search for one interesting car here and another there, they search out older car collectors who often have several cars in the garage or in the "lower 40."

Here's how they lucked onto a multiple gold mine:

"We were riding down the road one day and went past an old homestead,"

After removing the rubbish, this is what they found. Bill McKinnon, who has owned the car since 1967, wasn't interested in selling, but said that he enjoyed meeting Keith and his father, Don, and that they could come visit any time they liked. *Tom Cotter*

said Don. "We had driven past the place many times, but this time the garage door was open, and inside we saw a 1969 Camaro.

"A nice older gentleman spoke to us for a long time. It turns out he was a retired engineer from AT&T in Burlington, North Carolina, near Elon, the town where we lived at the time. For many years, he would buy an interesting car, use it for a while, then put it up."

The gentleman had good taste; inside the garage and various carports that had not been visible from the road sat a 1969 Corvette, 1965 Mustang convertible, 1956 Ford Thunderbird, 1930 Model A Tudor, and two 1950 Fords, a coupe and a convertible.

Outside there were many, many more vehicles. Behind the garage sat three motor homes, three boats, several later Thunderbirds, a couple of Cougars, and some 1970s Camaros.

In what resembled an apple orchard toward the back of his property, sat at least 20 more cars that, according to Isley, had been there for 20 or more years. Included in that group were Cadillacs, Mercurys, Rancheros, some tractors, and a fairly nice 1949 Ford pickup.

"He had a compressor and some tools in a back garage," said Isley. "It seemed he liked to tinker.

"He showed us everything and enjoyed spending time with us. We were mostly interested in the Camaro for Keith, but he said he could never sell that car because, 'My wife would kill me.'"

They didn't know it at the time, but this would be the last time they would speak with the gentleman.

Don and Keith said thank you and departed. They waited six months, called the house and spoke to the man's wife.

"Yeah, I know he spoke to someone and showed you his cars, but nothing is ever going to be for sale," she said.

They waited six months and then called, and the wife told them the same thing.

Six months later when Don called, there was no answer. He found out through a man in town that the family had moved to Florida and actually sold the property but retained lifetime rights to keep the cars parked there.

Six more months and Don searched for the couple in Florida through the Internet. He wrote an email letter offering to help the couple get the cars running.

"We never heard from them," said Don.

The town of Burlington is in Alamance County. At the time, a new ordinance was passed that restricted property owners to no more than two unregistered cars visible from the road, and they had to be covered.

"When we made our semiannual phone call, the wife said that she knew of the new restriction, and that, 'We'll have to come up there to straighten it out,'" said Isley. "But we didn't hear from her again."

Once when Don and Keith were traveling to the 24 Hour Race at Daytona, they attempted to visit the couple in nearby Astor, Florida, near Deland on the St. John's River. But as usual, they left a message and never received a reply.

"We're about four and one half years into this relationship at this point, and we were still going nowhere," said Don. Or so he thought.

"The wife called and told us her son, who lived in Greensboro, wanted to talk to us. It turns out that the older gentleman had Alzheimer's disease and was unable to manage his affairs.

"She told us that the man who bought their Burlington property had paid them additional money so he could begin construction of a subdivision immediately, so the cars had to go."

When Don and Keith spoke to the son, he asked them to make a list of the cars they were interested in and how much they were willing to pay. Their list included the 1956 Thunderbird, the two 1950 Fords, the 1949 Ford pickup, and two Cougars. And of course, the Camaro.

"The son met us over there and we made him an offer on each car," he said. "He told us that his stepfather had purchased the '56 T-Bird in 1958 from Atwater Ford, the local Burlington Ford agency on Main Street. It had only fifty-six thousand four hundred miles on it.

"It was in nice condition even though the roof in the garage leaked on the car every time it rained.

"He told us he wanted a little more money than we offered him for the Thunderbird, but once we upped that, he agreed to sell us everything except the Camaro, which was a four-speed RS/SS. That car was given to him by his stepdad."

Finally, by March 2009, Isley was able to buy the collection's most desirable cars.

Out of the blue soon after the transaction, Don received a phone call from a man in Burlington. "I heard you bought a few of those old cars," he said. "I've been trying to buy that 1950 Ford convertible from him for twenty years, but that old bastard wouldn't sell it. I'd like to buy it from you if you're interested."

"So I decided to sell the Ford to him," said Don. "He bought it and has done a nice job on it.

"Funny thing was, when we started dragging cars out of there, lots of people would stop by there and tell us they'd been trying to buy these cars for thirty-five years.

"I sold the '49 Ford pickup to one guy who stopped by as we were loading up cars on trailers."

While the Isleys were loading up their stash, other collectors who had purchased cars from the son were also loading up cars. According to Don, one man bought all the Falcons and Rancheros, another bought all the pickup trucks.

"People were lined up there all day Saturday," said Don.

Of all the people who had attempted to purchase the collection of cars, it was Don and Keith Isley who had the patience and perseverance to see it through.

What a great gift a father can pass onto his son.

CHAPTER SIX

Veterans of the Tarmac Wars

Coming to Grips with
a Slippery Question

By Randy Leffingwell

This was a tale with the elements of a good John Grisham page-turner. An innocuous email set up the chase. There were dead mice on the floor and elephant ears in a paper sack. Barn doors at Pine Grove Farm were nailed and then lag-bolted shut. There was an eccentric, retired GM engineer with Horace E. Dodge's personal Hispano-Suiza and a large collection of elegant fireplaces and old church pews. A judge was involved; paperwork hinted that this entire mystery was his fault. On the eve of discovery, an ice storm nearly shut down Detroit and dropped a tree limb on the garage, blocking the doors from opening. And that didn't even begin to address the questions about what made the dusty black car and the tired red one so desirable.

One of the slipperiest questions in Corvette history is the one about Z06 convertibles. Most historians had agreed there probably were none. Initially, GM's product planners didn't even make them possible. The first four Z06 sport coupes appeared at the Los Angeles Times Three-Hour Invitational race at Riverside International Raceway on Saturday, October 13, 1962. A mandatory ingredient of the Z06 recipe was a 36-gallon gasoline tank that nearly filled the back of the split-window fastback. While a Z06 won, the Riverside race provided Chevrolet an unhappy glimpse of the future as Dave MacDonald fought off Bill Krause driving a lone Shelby A.C. Cobra. Both cars failed at the end of the first hour. Jerry Grant and Bob Bondurant each lost engines in their new Z06s. This left Doug Hooper to soldier alone for the last 90 minutes. Hooper's big-tank coupe swallowed 31 gallons of fuel in a 20-second pit stop and held off a Porsche to win the race.

It was a short honeymoon. For the remainder of the racing season, Corvettes chased Carroll Shelby's lightweight open cars unsuccessfully. This quickly prompted some racers, Dick Guldstrand among them, to ask if Chevrolet would build an open Z06. "They turned me down," Dick recalled, "and told me just to buy the parts and install them myself." The division's documents report it assembled 199 cars with the $1,818 option. The package required the 360-horsepower L84 fuel-injected 327-cubic-inch engine, M20 four-speed transmission, and G81 Posi-Traction. It provided stiffer springs and bushings, larger-diameter shock absorbers, the N03 36-gallon gasoline

Find the hidden garage door! Even the best barn-finder would have a challenge entering this building. But one of the rarest, most sought-after Corvettes in history had been parked in this garage since 1964. *George Prentice*

tank, and P48 cast-aluminum knockoff wheels mounted on special finned brake drums with sintered metallic brake linings and heavy duty brake springs. The drums had rubber scoops directing cool air through screened backing plates to internal cooling fans. A new dual-circuit master cylinder brake booster first appeared on the Z06s. The wheels suffered problems with porosity, leaking air through rim beads and even the castings, and they proved heavier than Zora Duntov had hoped they would be. It seems that Chevrolet delivered no cars with those knockoffs until the next model year. Planners dropped them from the Z06 package. After they realized most racers were willing to replace the fuel tank with one of their own choosing, Chevy removed that piece from the Z06 configuration as well. Ultimately, the division delivered only 63 Z06 cars with the large tanks installed.

In March 1963, in *Corvette News*, public relations staffer Joe Pike announced that the division had a change of heart. "With the introduction of the new [1963] Corvette, certain performance items were announced for sport coupes destined to enter performance meets. The items grouped under RPO Z06 were not initially released for convertibles. Increasing customer requests to have the special performance equipment option available for both the convertible and the sport coupe led Chevrolet distribution to announce the availability of a revised option for both 1963 models."

Without the wheels and big tank, Chevrolet quoted the new package price at $1,293.95, plus either $4,257 for the coupe or $4,037 for the convertible.

His GM employee discount meant that Waino L. Husko would get the Z06 option essentially as a no-extra charge package. Wayne, as colleagues called him, was Finnish and had joined the General Motors Tech Center staff from Ford as a 37-year-old design engineer in 1947. He worked in prototype engineering, making real features work properly on Harley Earl's and then Bill Mitchell's show cars, design studies, and pre-production models.

His position inside GM's design center gave him opportunities to meet other auto industry movers and shakers. A growing

With just 7,500 miles on the odometer, the only Z06 Corvette convertible ever built was parked because its owner was about to lose his driver's license in 1964—too many speeding tickets. Thus, a near-perfect time capsule was preserved. *George Prentice*

friendship with an always cash-strapped Horace E. Dodge Jr. put Husko in the position to acquire Horace's father's 1920 Hispano-Suiza H-6 (with his initials still on the driver's door), a 1934 Standard Swallow SS1 saloon (the Jaguar predecessor), and later the 1938 Packard V-12 limousine that Dodge's widow owned.

Wayne's love of cars led him to add a 1903 curved dash Oldsmobile and a 1905 Cadillac to his growing collection. In 1959, after the tech center finished with it, Husko acquired the 1953 Corvette No. 8, a car that engineering had used to test engines and improve handling and rear suspension. From there, it suffered a hard life. In Wayne's possession, it got hit twice and he repainted it red. But when he acquired cars, he didn't let them go.

In early May 1963, he visited Jefferson Chevrolet and ordered a black convertible with Joe Pike's Z06 option. (He had tried to do this the previous

Facing rising medical costs for their aging father, family members had no option but to sell their dad's beloved 1963 Corvette. Corvette experts were brought in to appraise the car as it sat in the decrepit garage. *George Prentice*

October, but, as with Guldstrand, Chevrolet kicked his order back.) This time it went through. Early in June, E. C. Buss, Chevrolet's assistant plant distribution manager at St. Louis assembly, wrote to Wayne, noting that "we have received your order and we're glad you're taking advantage of the General Motors employee buyer's program." Buss personally signed the note. A week later, on June 10, he wrote again:

"Your Corvette, order 5283, Zone order D-170, dealer code 44-236, model 867, will be released for production June 14. Expect to ship early week June 17, 1963." When Jefferson Chevrolet called to tell him his car was in, his window sticker read $5,926.42, including an AM-FM pushbutton radio, the auxiliary hardtop, 6.70-15 whitewall tires, and, oddly, the 3.08 rear axle. His discount, $1,341.36, cut the price to $4,585.09, easily absorbing the additional charge for the Z06 option. He put $2,509.99 down and financed the balance at $72.55 a month for 36 months. At the time, Husko was 52 years old. He was working brutally long hours preparing Mitchell's special Sting Rays for New York, Chicago, and other auto shows around the United States and the rest of the world.

One night, he came out to find the black convertible missing. His car had just 1,600 miles on it. When police recovered it in Mississippi, All-State, his insurance company, had to face repairs to windows and vent windows, the ignition lock, the left door lock, the gearshift linkage, and many of the wires passing through the firewall. Barely 1,200 miles later, he had to replace the clutch, probably destroyed by the joy-riding car thieves fighting a close-ratio transmission with a high-ratio final drive.

Wayne had his own problems with the car. As anyone who has driven Corvettes with sintered metallic brake shoes can attest, stopping the car before the brakes are hot is a difficult task that can become a terrifying challenge. When he returned the car for service, Jefferson's service manager scrawled across the work order, "This car should not be driven. Not safe to drive. Owner risks if driven." He ordered new brake drums and shoes. A week later, Jefferson installed the second-generation finned brake drums and a new shoe set under factory warranty.

Waino Husko took to blowing off steam with GM's styling chief Bill Mitchell and others tech center staffers, racing through the streets. This form of stress relief introduced additional problems that led to his working knowledge of the names of many police officers in several communities. Husko's friend Ron Skonieczny of McComb, Michigan, explained how it worked.

"The cops would just wait at the gate on Mound Road for Mitchell and the others to come out of the gates. Mitchell would take home the Mako Sharks or other cars. He had lots of points on his license." Another friend from GM design, George Prentice, knew more of the story.

"Wayne used his car as daily transportation. And he and some other guys had outrageous driving styles, a lifestyle highly promoted by Bill Mitchell, who had crashed a number of cars himself. They were real lead foots. He was not a bad driver, just a fast driver."

In late 1964, with 18 points on Wayne's license, the judge in Wayne County presented him the option of parking the car for a while or losing his license. Wayne filled the tank with high-test Ethyl and drove the Z06 into the garage. It had barely 7,500 miles on it. In 1970 he and his wife, Jen, bought Pine Grove Farm in Romeo, and he moved his still-growing car collection from his garage on West Grand Boulevard into his new barn. He parked the 1953 No. 8 a few feet away from his 1963 Z06.

Husko retired from GM in 1975 and began the next phase of his life. For years he had been rescuing decorative architectural pieces from Detroit's Indian Village mansions and the city's old churches before wrecking balls leveled them. He continued piling newfound treasures around his older automotive treasures, slowly filling his garage and barn and then additional warehouses.

"Waino was hard to explain," Ron Skonieczny recalled. "He collected and collected and kept storing and storing, putting things in buildings, but he never shared his collections with anyone. He had a lot of warehouses around Detroit. We thought he should have a museum or an antique store; he just bought things and stored them. He was just a secretive guy who collected things just to collect. Whenever he went collecting junk, he'd put on ratty overalls and he smoked cigars. He had a green, a blue, and a red Corvair van, each one with side gates to making loading the stuff easier."

For another quarter century, he hoarded old cash registers, a 1969 Pontiac Grand Prix, gas pumps, a 1985 Cadillac Eldorado, fine wood furniture, a 1986 Suburban, elegant clocks, a 1990 Chevy SS454 pickup, mechanical toys, and a 1957 yellow and white Chevy Bel-Air. Then he began to slow down.

His two daughters brought in daytime help for their aging father, and they faced the fact that by his late 80s, it was likely he never again would drive his two Corvettes. They contacted GM design center staffer George Prentice, who himself owned a modified 1954 Corvette. Facing Wayne's mounting medical costs, they asked Prentice to help them sell the 1953 and 1963 Corvettes. Prentice broadcast an email to 30 names he knew within the Corvette world, and Noland Adams forwarded it to another dozen, including a new acquaintance in Salt Lake City who had expressed sincere interest in acquiring a 1953.

Bill Shipp was a newcomer to the Corvette world and the car collecting hobby. He'd bought a 2002 brand-new, visited the Monterey Historics the year it honored Corvette, and quickly embraced the passion. He acquired a 1958, and his friend Corey Peterson began to educate him on other collectibles. When Prentice's email arrived on Peterson's computer along with photos of two very dirty, rough cars literally buried in a barn in Michigan, neither man got too excited.

"The photos were so bad," Bill recalled, "and the condition of the [1953] car appeared so rough that literally the photos turned most people off. It was under an inch or more of white dust." Both men agreed to pass. But then Prentice broadcast a new email and that piqued their interest:

"Please submit a final bid for one or both vehicles, higher or lower than the asking price. We are asking $85,000 for the 1953 Corvette, number ES128. We are asking $60,000 for the 1963 Corvette. We are asking $145,000 for the pair." Prentice promised to keep bids and sale prices confidential. Neither Shipp nor Peterson could believe the values these cars were reaching based on the photos. They knew that at that time, in early 2003, they could find beautifully restored fuel-injected 1963 convertibles for less than $50,000. They asked George to shoot some additional pictures of each car. Fortunately for Bill and Corey, because they alone asked for more pictures, Prentice sent the new set only to them. What they saw prompted them to call George. Standing near the 1963, George got down on his knees and looked under the nose of the car. He told Corey it had funny front wheels, like a gear on each one. "Like a ring gear?" Corey asked. "Yes, I'd say so," George replied. "I didn't know what I was looking at," he explained later.

Finned brake drums were uncommon on 1963s. Knowledgeable collectors knew of only 199 sets in existence, all of them on Z06s. When Prentice lifted the hood and described the brake master cylinder with two lines rather than one, Peterson knew then and there that he and Shipp were going to Michigan. But on the day of the flight, Detroit got slammed with an ice storm that nearly shuttered the city and dropped a large tree limb across the door, hiding the 1963. Peterson, anxious to see the black convertible, literally manhandled the limb out of the way so they could go in. With their suspicions and hopes rising as the miles passed under their plane, Peterson and Shipp had plotted a strategy in which Shipp was to show more interest in the 1953 so Corey could climb around the 1963 by himself. It was not hard for Bill; up to that point, he still was more interested in owning the early car.

Once in the barn, George took Bill off to see the 1953. Corey opened the 1963 and rummaged around. In the storage wells beneath the seats, he found the "elephant ears," the shrouds that mounted on the inside of the front brake drums to force in cool air. These still were in the paper sack in which they'd been packaged at the factory. Hoping Prentice had not noticed, he jammed them back in the bag and hid them in the compartment, aching to tell Shipp what this car was, but not wanting to tip his hand to Prentice. Another bidder from New York already had visited the cars with George, and he had come to identical conclusions. He also chose to remain silent to Prentice. Peterson felt similar excitement with the 1953 when, standing beside it, he called John Amgwert, an acknowledged expert on the earliest cars. This one had been used hard, but the red-painted 1953 bore significant engineering modifications, making it very desirable despite the fact that countless field mice had made it a home and several had died inside in it.

Over the next two days, Shipp, Peterson, and Prentice returned to the garage and the barn each day, helping to clear the clutter to see the cars better. Prentice had urged the daughters to let him push the cars out and clean them up, knowing that a better appearance could as much as double the bidding prices. They refused, worrying that their father might see people crawling around his cars and get upset.

Each night Bill and Corey massaged their strategy for how they would end up with both Corvettes. Bidders from the East Coast had begun to weigh in. Corey had heard George on his cell phone telling callers, including the knowledgeable New Yorker, that values continued to climb. "The bidding was really strange," Prentice recalled. "People called me up throwing money at me. Every call raised their bid by a thousand or five thousand dollars. So I set a deadline so they all could submit what they wanted pay for one car, the other, or both."

Corey Peterson knew many of them, and he recognized that their resources would make either car expensive to buy. A Chevrolet dealer and significant Corvette collector in Warren, Michigan, Fred Rinke, already had boasted to friends that no matter what he had to pay, he would own the 1953.

The night before the bidding deadline, Corey wrote Bill's offer. As Bill described it later, "He effortlessly spent a large sum of my money."

Shipp and Peterson had put in several days by now, inspecting the cars and often sharing meals with George Prentice. Because of the friendship they had developed, Prentice and his wife had invited Shipp and Peterson to their home for the bid opening. Several had come in by email, all in the proper form that George had asked. As Prentice revealed the numbers, Bill was beginning to think he'd won the sale. Then Prentice opened Rinke's handwritten bid. Fred had not exactly followed the form. He simply had written, "I bid . . ." and a very large number followed.

George paled.

At that point, Bill sized up the dilemma and offered an out. While he had bid for each car separately and for the two together as requested, from the perspective he had gained during the week, the black 1963 convertible was more unique, if that's possible, than an engineering staff 1953 model.

"All right, George," he told Prentice, "if you have to sell the 1953 to Fred Rinke, then you have to sell the 1963 to me." Tension fell away; the deal was done. With power of attorney granted to him for Wayne's daughters, George signed a bill of sale and Bill wrote a deposit check. The balance transferred the next morning electronically.

Husko's daughters Julie and Mary met Bill and Corey for the first time in the cold outside the garage. Bill recalled that it was apparent to him the two had been crying. These cars had been among their father's treasures, and it was hard to accept that the 91-year-old man inside the farmhouse a short distance away never would enjoy them again.

A flatbed drove away with the Z06, headed to Steve Pasteiner's Advance Automotive Technologies facilities in nearby Rochester Hills. Pasteiner had worked with Husko, was a friend of Prentice's, and he had agreed to arrange transport for the car to Salt Lake. When he saw it and when Corey pointed out the significant parts, Pasteiner recalled that there always had been a rumor that Wayne Husko had bought such a car. But no one ever had seen it. No one, except perhaps the late Bill Mitchell and a handful of local police.

Being the discoverer and owner of something rare and special makes you a target. At a National Corvette Restorers Society meeting in Zion National Monument soon after the Z06 arrived in Utah, Bill heard criticism of his car. Some experts said it wasn't what Shipp claimed, that it was an engineering special, similar to what Husko's colleagues had done to ES128, the white-then-red 1953 No. 8. Without the documentation, Shipp could only listen and bristle. Waino Husko died on December 23, 2003, and once family members got to sort his papers, they began forwarding irrefutable documentation that let the new owner and experts alike put a firm grip on the slippery question and silence the skeptics at last: Yes, there was at least one 1963 Z06 convertible. And GM engineer Waino Husko had ordered it, bought it, driven it, enjoyed it, never even bothered to remove the hardtop, and finally parked it in his barn.

The Sebring Alfa in the Chicken Coop

Not all barn finds are secret. Several years ago my friend Jim Maxwell and I purchased a 32,000-mile 1967 Shelby GT500 that many enthusiasts knew about.

"Oh, you're wasting your time, Bob will never sell," they said. Yet today Jim and I own one of the most original big-block Shelbys on the planet. It called for relationship building, not a "Here's my best offer; take it or leave it" mentality.

Jim McNeil of Bayport, New York, had a similar experience after hearing about a rare Alfa Romeo SZ that had been sitting in a chicken coop outside of Baltimore.

"It was a known car," said McNeil, who along with his wife, Sandra, own and race a number of desirable historic sports car. "But it was one of those stories of the owner who always said he was going to restore it. But he never did."

Lots of enthusiasts knew about the little Alfa coupe, probably for as long as 35 years. When new it was sent by the factory to a Northport, New York–based team run by Lou Comito, otherwise known as Mr. Alfa. Actually, the factory sent three Alfas to be campaigned at the 1961 Sebring 12-Hour race by Mr. Alfa's team.

"He juiced up the motors with hotter camshafts," said McNeil. "They really produced some decent horsepower. If you wanted to race an Alfa, you couldn't leave the 1290cc engine alone if you wanted to go fast."

And go fast they did. Driver of a sister Alfa SZ in the 1961 Sebring race was Tommy O'Brien. He told McNeil more recently that "It was the fastest car at Sebring." Actually, it wasn't the fastest car, but with drivers Harry Theodoracopulos and Comito, the No. 57 Alfa finished 39th out of a 64-car field that included more powerful cars like Ferraris, Corvettes, and Porsches.

After Sebring, the car was sold to Lazy Vizelli, who continued to race it for five or six more years. In the early 1970s, the Alfa was sold to Ray Cuomo of Long Island before being sold to Ed Williamson of Brooklyn.

"Williamson knew it had a trick motor in it, so he bought it and pulled the motor out to put in his Veloce Spider race car, which he ran in the early VSCCA races for a number of years," said McNeil.

After changing hands a few more times—to owners in Tennessee, Massachusetts, and back to New York—the rare little coupe was purchased

The Victress S1A fiberglass sports car that once graced the lobby of the Petersen Publishing offices in Los Angeles is now in the process of being restored by new owner Guy Dirkin. The car was built by *Motor Trend* magazine's Technical Editor Fred Bodley and was featured in the magazine. *Guy Dirkin*

by Frank Salemi of Connecticut. Salemi was a member of the Alfa Romeo Owners Club, and he intended to restore the car. But it sat.

Eventually, McNeil began thinking about buying an SZ coupe after another Alfa was involved in an on-track altercation.

"I've always wanted a Z," he said. "We were racing an Alfa Sprint coupe at the time, and we got into a fender bender. So that's when I decided to look for an SZ."

Through his crew chief at KTR Racing in Massachusetts, Andy Funk, McNeil heard about an SZ that was somewhere in Connecticut. He started a search for Sameli, who by then had moved to the Baltimore area, which complicated the search.

McNeil put the word out among his Alfa buddies that he was looking for an SZ that had vanished, when one day he got a phone call from an enthusiast from Baltimore.

"He told me he knew of a coupe that was sitting in a chicken coop," said McNeil. "But he also said it wasn't for sale, that the owner was going to restore it.

"Well it was the same car I had been trying to find in Connecticut, but

Loaded with Bondo and neglected in this chicken coop, the whereabouts of this Alfa was well-known among enthusiasts. But the owner refused to sell until Long Island collector Jim McNeil convinced him he would restore the car back to its 1961 race condition. *Jim and Sandra McNeil collection*

the leads had all dried up. It was obvious, though, that after owning the car from 1973 until 2000, if he didn't restore the car in that time, he wasn't going to restore it."

He called Salemi and told him he was a serious buyer.

"I had to convince Salemi that we were the right people to own and restore that car," he said. He was successful and was offered the car.

"He sold it to us pretty inexpensively, but we had to invest a lot into it," he said. "It wasn't as nice as it had appeared. You could almost stand on the ground while inside the car; it was that bad."

KTR Crew Chief and General Manager Funk agrees. "It was clear that the car had been wrapped around a tree at some point in its life," he said Funk. "It wasn't straight at all. It was loaded with Bondo, probably from a quickie restoration done sometime in the 1960s.

"It had shiny paint, but once we stripped it off, there wasn't much left."

Funk and his crew took more than two years to restore the tired race car into the condition it was when it first entered Sebring 40 years earlier.

Since then, with Sandra McNeil driving, the car has competed in vintage races at Lime Rock, Connecticut, and at the 2009 Goodwood Revival in England.

The McNeils are pleased with the newest addition to their race car collection. "They're not furniture, we like to use our cars," said McNeil.

Even Funk, who got many bloody knuckles while restoring the coupe, has warm feelings about the car.

"It's a neat little car now," he said. "We brought it back from the dead."

After a several-year restoration at KTR Racing in Ayer, Massachusetts, the car made its vintage racing debut here in 2009 at the prestigious Goodwood Revival in England with Sandra McNeil behind the wheel. *Jim and Sandra McNeil collection*

The Hog Farmers'
Fuel-Injected Mouse Den

By Bill Connell

"It's not for sale!"

How many times have we heard these as the first words out of an old car owner's mouth after we rang the doorbell?

This is what Bill the Farmer said when asked if the old Corvette in his barn was for sale. Bill was a hog farmer in rural Ohio. In his younger days, he raised a lot of hell street-racing and drag racing various hot rods in and around his rural hometown. As he got older, though, he became both reclusive and a "hoarder" of all things mechanical.

Inside various barns and outbuildings around his farm, Bill stored an assortment of Corvettes, farm tractors, pre–World War II motorcycles, and literally tons of assorted junk. Bill Connell was the one who asked Bill if he could purchase the above-mentioned Corvette.

Connell was intrigued with the car and its No. 4007 serial number because he believed it was one of the long-lost serial No. 4007 cars, one of only 43 Corvette "airbox" racers that Chevrolet built for serious road racing in 1957.

The rare airbox was raced regularly during the 1957 SCCA season by original owner Bill Howe and his racing buddy Jack Knab. At the car's first race, in Cumberland, Maryland, the car finished an impressive third after Corvettes driven by Dick Thompson and Carroll Shelby. *Bill Connell collection*

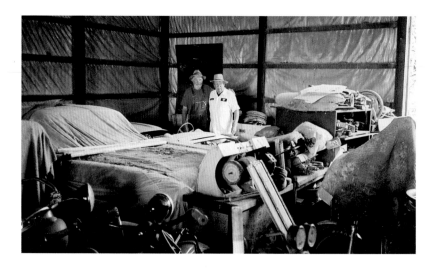

Having been buried for decades inside Bill the Farmer's barn, the rare Corvette is barely visible under a cover and mountains of rubbish. Bill the Farmer is on the left, and Joel Lauman is on the right. *Bill Connell collection*

In January 1957, General Motors announced the car's development at a special Sports Car Club of America (SCCA) meeting in Warren, Michigan. Corvettes ordered with the RPO 579E option would be fitted with a competition suspension, which included heavy-duty springs, a quicker steering ratio, heavy duty shocks, larger wheels, and special ceramic drum brake linings with cooling ducts. But the major modification was the installation of a cold airbox, which captured cooler, higher-density outside air and forced it into the Rochester fuel-injection unit. The same air was also supposed to aid cooling to the rear brakes.

"General Motors told the amateur racers in attendance that if any of them ordered the car during the convention, they would guarantee delivery in time to compete in the Cumberland, Maryland, road races that May," said Connell. Several versions of the Corvette would be driven by professional racer drivers that March in Sebring, with the team of Dick Thompson and Gaston Andrey finishing in a hard-fought 12th place overall, first in class against a strong field of Maseratis, Ferraris, Jaguars, and Porsches. Interestingly, at that race, the airboxes were removed because they contributed to overheating of the left-rear brakes.

"The front brakes had funnels that resembled elephant ears to cool them," said Connell. "But the rear brakes were a different story. The right rear brake

Sunlight at last! The 1957 Corvette is pushed out of the barn for the first time in 28 years. It had been stripped of paint and some components, but a shopping bag full of cash separated Bill the Farmer from his long-term project. *Bill Connell collection*

was cooled by a large hose, and that worked fine, but the left rear brake shared cool air with the engine intake.

"When the engine was driven hard, it required all the cool air that the airbox could capture, which caused the left-side rear brakes to badly overheat. There just wasn't enough air in the box for both duties."

Anyway, at the January SCCA meeting in Detroit, two racers were particularly excited: Bill Howe and Jack Knab. Howe owned a Chevrolet dealership in Middletown, Ohio, and on weekends he raced in amateur sports car races. Knab was his racing buddy. At the conclusion of the meeting, Howe plunked down his deposit and was promised the car in plenty of time to make the May 19, 1957, SCCA National event in Cumberland.

He waited and waited, hoping he'd get the car soon enough to at least practice driving it in a lesser event. What Howe didn't know was that General Motors, along with Ford and Chrysler, voluntarily ceased participating in racing events and marketing high-performance automobiles. Chevrolet's head engineer Ed Cole had the factories in a tizzy as they attempted to get their racing programs closed down before the end of June.

"There was such tension to complete the cars that engineers sourced prototype parts from the engineering department just to complete the cars on time," says Connell.

Mike Lauman, who helped his dad, Joel, restore the Corvette, stands proudly next to the car as it was displayed in the ballroom of the Bloomington Gold 1957 Special Collection. *Bill Connell collection*

On May 16, word finally came that his Corvette was completed. Howe and Knab jumped on a plane and flew to the St. Louis assembly plant to take delivery. They quickly signed the papers and headed east. They drove through the night, as they had only two days to drive the new Corvette to Maryland, change tires, prep the car, and practice before the Sunday race.

That Sunday's feature race has been viewed as Corvette's "coming out party," because the brand dominated the field with the "Flying Dentist," Dr. Dick Thompson, winning, and champion racer driver Carroll Shelby finishing second, both driving 1957 Corvettes. And amateur driver Howe finished third, attesting to the race-worthiness of No. 4007 with the RPO 579E package. With that, Howe jumped in his car and drove back to Ohio so he could be at work on Monday morning.

Howe continued to race No. 4007 for the rest of the season and even assisted GM in early brake testing of the new sintered metallic competition brakes, which would be offered to racers in 1960.

At the end of the 1957 season, No. 4007 was retired from road racing. Howe parked the car on his used car lot as he awaited the delivery of his new 1958 Corvette with the RPO 684 competition package.

According to Connell, No. 4007 went through three more owners and accumulated about 41,000 miles—much of it one-quarter mile at a time—before going into a 28-year hibernation. But none of the owners subsequent to Howe knew of the car's significant racing heritage.

This is where Bill the Farmer comes in.

In the 1970s, Bill the Farmer, who was a longtime drag racer, decided he wanted an early fuel-injected Corvette. He stumbled across No. 4007, which to him was just an abused old Corvette. He bought it and partially stripped it to begin restoration.

Bill stripped the paint and removed many parts before losing interest and pushing the car in the corner of the barn, where it sat for the next 28 years. During that time, the Corvette became increasingly crowded in the barn as Bill continued to purchase and store additional vehicles and machinery.

An old drag racing buddy of his, Joel Lauman, was one of the few people who saw the Corvette when his friend bought it. Lauman, a Corvette restorer, believed the car was an authentic airbox racer, which didn't seem to faze Bill.

"I'm going to finish the restoration when I have the time," he'd say.

Lauman called his friend Connell and told him of his suspicion that the car was possibly a rare racer. The two decided to try and take a look at it.

Bill was becoming increasingly reclusive. He was a well-armed big man who could lift engines in and out of cars without the use of an engine hoist—not the sort who attracts folks just to drive up to his farm and knock on the door.

"You had to arrange your visit in advance so Bill would put away the guns and dogs," said Connell. Phone calls went unanswered, so Lauman and Connell left notes in Bill's mailbox, hoping to get an appointment.

Eventually, Bill invited Lauman over "To pay tribute to Jack." In other words, the two would sit on the porch on Sunday afternoons, sip Jack Daniels, and bench race. Just when Lauman thought he was making progress, Bill mentioned he was still planning to restore the Corvette when he had some time. "And it's definitely not for sale!"

As the years passed, Bill's health began to deteriorate to the point where even he admitted he was no longer capable of restoring the Corvette.

In 2005, Lauman finally said to Bill: "Bill, you're never going to restore that car. I know a guy [Connell] who will pay you for the car and allow me to restore it." Bill agreed, but only after Lauman promised he would arrange for Bill to drive the car upon completion. That sealed the deal, or so Lauman and Connell thought.

"So the next week I went out to the farm and gave him a Kroger shopping bag filled with cash," Connell said. "That satisfied him."

Bill invited Lauman and Connell into the master bedroom of his old farmhouse, where he reached under the bed, pulled out a briefcase, and removed the title. Before handing the title to the new owner, Bill said, "You know, you are the first man to ever set foot inside my bedroom."

It took at least two days for Bill to dig out all the Corvette's pieces that were hidden around the farmhouse.

Once the car was removed from the farm, Connell began to take account of what he had just purchased. "At this point, I knew I had an airbox car, but many of the experts said that it wasn't; that the serial number was too early."

Lauman and Connell decided not to restore or even disassemble No. 4007, but instead take thousands of photos and attempt to document the car properly.

"Joel was going to Corvette Carlisle, so I asked him to bring the distributor with him to have Ken Kayser take a look at it," said Connell. "Ken, a former senior GM engineer, is considered the dean of old Corvettes.

"Kayser looked at the distributor and asked, 'Where did you get this? The codes say this is an engineering piece. This is unusual; I'd like to learn more about this car.' He asked if he could come down to see the car sometime."

As Connell explains, Kayser conducted a forensic engineering audit on No. 4007 and was underneath the car for at least two hours. When he crawled out from under the car, Kayser proclaimed, "This is the real deal with this low serial number. It was probably the pilot for the airbox-series cars.

"I need to do more research, but in the meantime, please don't show anyone the car until we have more documentation," said Kayser. "And don't throw anything away. We have a lot of questions to answer before you begin pulling it apart."

Kayser, along with a number of Corvette experts, including Joe Trybulec and Jack Knab, finally concluded that No. 4007 was the original "pilot" car for all subsequent airbox cars and is the earliest known in the series.

Corvette No. 4007 went through a comprehensive two-year restoration and was completed in time for the 50th anniversary of the 1957 Corvette at the annual Bloomington Gold event. Connell's Corvette shared the special collection stage with several other airbox racers and other 1957 models of special note. In 2008, No. 4007 was awarded the Bloomington Gold certificate, as well as the National Corvette Restorers Society Top Flight Award. The car has also appeared at the Cinncinati Concours, where it was awarded Best Corvette, at the Amelia Island Concours d'Elegance, and on the Discovery Channel's one-of-a-kind "How Stuff Works" series.

These days, the car is absolutely beautiful, but Connell reminds admirers that this car hasn't always looked so proper. "This is a barn-find car in the truest sense, because we had to remove a family of mice who had been happily living in the airbox!"

Uncle Eddie's
Backyard Gasser Ford

Dave Redman didn't want to upset his Uncle Eddie. Uncle Eddie has been a traditional hot rodder from the time he was a youth, and he tried to convince his nephew Dave to build himself a street rod. But Dave wasn't into street rods.

"I was more into 1950s to 1970s high-performance Fords," said Redman, 48. "Especially Shelby Mustangs, Boss Mustangs, and old race cars," such as the 1970 Boss 429 drag car he bought in 1990.

"This 429 car had never been registered for the street," he said. "It had originally been purchased and raced by Sam and Rick Auxier of Maryland." The Boss Mustang first competed with the 429-cubic-inch engine in Super Stock/C, then raced in A/Super Modified with a 351 Cleveland.

Redman started competing in nostalgic drag races with the Mustang, and the car was featured in several magazines. This whetted Redman's appetite to own an even older drag car, which was certainly not the street rod that Uncle Eddie wanted him to build.

Early gasser-class cars captivated Redman's attention.

"Even though most people think of a 1941 Willys coupe or a 1948 Anglia when they hear the word 'gasser,' my mind goes to a 1955 or 1956 Chevy two-door sedan," he said. "When I was investigating information on my Boss through old magazines and video, I got fired up with those old shoebox gassers.

"But all my Ford buddies would never let me live down owning a Chevy, so I figured that even though finding a Ford gasser is as rare as hen's teeth, I could probably build a replica."

But other car projects got in the way of pursuing that idea.

One of Redman's friends found a 1955 Chevy gasser with all the lettering still on it. He said he'd love to find one like that, only a Ford. After he showed up at the York US-30 Muscle Car Madness event in Pennsylvania, he saw a barn-find 1956 Ford gasser, and his mind was made up.

"That car was a real time capsule," said Redman. "Seeing that car really tripped my trigger to find one like it."

Uncle Eddie called, still trying to convince his nephew to build a street rod. Finally, Redman told him that he wasn't interested in the street rod, but if he ever stumbled across a 1955 to 1957 Ford gasser-style sedan, he would buy it. He didn't think his uncle would remember, until a couple of years later.

It was during a tough time for the Redman family. Redman's father was in the last stages of mesothelioma, a form of lung cancer due to asbestos exposure.

In 1965, when this photo was taken, Don Hedrick's Auto Muffler King of Newport News, Virginia, built custom headers for this Ford, campaigned at the time by Dick Perdue. The car raced with a 390- and then a 427-cubic-inch engine at Virginia drag strips. *Dave Redman collection*

He and his brother Paul attended the NHRA Nationals in Petersburg, Virginia, but it was hard to enjoy themselves knowing their dad's condition was rapidly deteriorating. He regularly made the three-hour trip to Colonial to visit his dad in the hospital. During one trip, he stopped by his boyhood home to visit his mom. During the visit, his mom said that her brother, Uncle Eddie, called and asked to have Redman call back when he had a chance.

"She said he said something about a 1956 Ford," said Redman. "But with my dad in the hospital, I really didn't feel like calling and talking about cars. But I decided to call him back anyway before taking the three-hour drive home."

"Hey, I found you a '56 Ford with no engine or transmission," said Uncle Eddie. "The frame is rusty but the body is great."

Redman figured that with a rusty frame, the body was also rusted, but had been patched up.

"I just wasn't very interested," said Redman. "Then Uncle Eddie said, 'Do you remember Dick Perdue? It's his old car.'"

Redman didn't know Dick Perdue, but had heard of him. Redman believed Perdue helped a local drag racer with his 1965 Shelby GT350, sponsored by Bowditch Ford in Newport News.

After sitting under a tarp in Perdue's brother Bob's backyard, Redman was able to purchase the one-time gasser. He is sympathetically restoring the car, but swears it will not lose the wonderful patina it has achieved. *Dave Redman*

Uncle Eddie kept describing the car. "The only thing I can see that's wrong with the car is that the rear fender wells are cut out," he said.

Redman perked up. "The rear fenders are cut out? Why, did he race it or something?" Redman asked.

"Yeah, it was his old drag car," said Uncle Eddie.

Redman was all ears. The Ford had belonged to Perdue's brother, Bob, for the past 35 years, who had come to the realization that he probably would never get around to fixing it up and was putting it up for sale.

Arrangements were made for Redman and Uncle Eddie to see the car on Monday.

But Redman's dad passed away Sunday night, so the Ford was temporarily forgotten. Making the funeral arrangements, the viewing, and the funeral itself kept Redman and his family occupied all week, but he made arrangements to see the old Ford the following Saturday afternoon.

"Believe me, I needed something to look forward to that week," he said. "My dad was a real car nut, and as kids, he's take us to gymkhanas, drag races, and stock car races." Redman felt his father would have wanted him to look at the Ford.

After the funeral, he went to Uncle Eddie's house and changed into old clothes. The two drove over to Bob's house to see the Ford. They walked into the backyard where the red 1956 Ford sedan had sat, covered with a tarp, for many years. What he saw was the car he had been dreaming of for many years. It was a retired gasser with radiused rear fender openings, flat black front fenders, and a hole in the hood where a scoop had once been installed.

"Once the tarp was lifted, I saw a pretty dusty and weathered car, but it was in pretty good shape," said Redman. "I looked underneath and the floorboards and rocker panels were pretty solid. It had a Ford nine-inch rear end housing and Thunderbolt-style ladder bars."

Uncle Eddie showed him the rusted frame, but it was actually just the front crossmember, which was fairly common during 1950s Fords.

"It was a real race car from back in the day, and it had been relatively well-prepared," said Redman. "I already decided I was going to buy the car unless the price was outrageously high."

He continued to circulate around the car and his passion for it grew. On the driver's-side window vent was a "NASCAR Drag Class Winner" decal; when he opened the driver's door, he noticed it had a genuine Shelby GT350 wooden steering wheel with a Cobra center cap and cast hub.

"As a diehard GT350 fanatic, all I could think was, 'I guess I'm going to have to buy this car,'" he said.

"I asked Bob how much he wanted for the car, realizing it would be obscene to beat him up over the price. He said he'd like to get one thousand two hundred dollars, and I told him, 'You just sold your car.' Then Bob started to tell me the tale of the car."

Apparently his brother, Dick, was a mechanic at Bowditch Ford in the 1960s and early 1970s. One day Dick was working on a truck in the dealership when another mechanic reached in to start the truck, not realizing it was still in gear. The truck lurched forward and pinned Dick against the wall. His legs were broken, and as a settlement from the dealership, Dick received the 1956 Ford plus sponsorship to build and race it. Dick built the car originally with a 390-cubic-inch engine, but later changed to a 427. He raced the car regularly at Suffolk Raceway and Virginia Beach Dragway. When Dick started racing stock cars, he parked the Ford and eventually sold it to his brother Bob.

After Redman bought the car, he ran into Don Hedrick, the retired owner of Auto Muffler King in Newport News. "Don used to build custom headers and do roll cage work in addition to standard exhaust systems," said Redman. "I told him about the car and he said, 'Yeah, I remember that car. In 1965, I built headers for it.'

"He showed me photos he took of the car, and there it was with real good shots of 'Sponsored by Bowditch Ford' signs painted on the rear quarter panels and 'Headers by Muffler King' on the front fenders.

"I found out more of this car's racing history in three days than I did about my Boss 429 in ten years," he said.

Redman is now in the process of giving the retired Ford gasser a "sympathetic" restoration. Even though he would prefer to build a 406- or 427-cubic-inch engine for it, he couldn't find an affordable block, so he will install a 390. It will be backed up by a top-loader four-speed from a 1965 Galaxy.

"I'm still looking for an intake manifold and a set of Ansen wheels for it," he said. "And I've already found a set of green-faced Stewart-Warner gauges and a period Sun tachometer."

In the interim, Redman purchased a set of old Fenton Hawk wheels, which were manufactured by Mickey Thompson and resemble the Radar wheel style, but he is nervous about their quality.

The front fenders were still in fiberglass gel coat, so Redman is having them painted with a patina to match the rest of the body.

Redman said the Ford ran with Thunderbolt seats in the 1960s, but since those are difficult to locate, he'll use Mercury Cyclone seats, which look and fit fine.

"I want to keep the car as 'survivor-ish' as possible, and I only plan to paint it where it is absolutely necessary," he said.

"It was something to stumble onto a car that was almost exactly what I was looking for."

Thanks to Uncle Eddie.

The Twin-Engine Beer-Find Dragster

Many times, too much beer can lead to something bad. In rare cases, it can lead to something good.

Scott Mason of West Virginia was visiting buddy Karl Kelly's garage one Saturday; the two drank beer and talked cars. Kelly had been a drag racer and always had great stories about cars and races.

One beer led to another, and eventually nature called. Mason walked around the back of the garage to relieve himself and discovered more than the privacy he sought. He found an old dragster chassis lying in the weeds.

"Karl bought the car out of *National Dragster* for seven thousand five hundred dollars in the 1980s and bracket-raced it around the South for five or six years," said Mason, 50, of Charleston. "He never did very good with it, so eventually he stripped it and just dumped the chassis behind his building."

Drag racing had brought Kelly and Mason together as friends. At the time, Mason was racing a 1967 Plymouth, but Kelly preferred the faster rail-type dragsters.

"Kelly had been a motorcycle chopper guy, who would beat up guys for the fun of it," said Mason. "He was the kind of guy who played with dynamite and hand grenades." Kelly decided the loud noise and potential danger of drag racing was a much more "gentle" way to spend his free time.

"It was just lying in the weeds. It was basically the bare frame and nothing else. So I asked Karl if I could have it and he said, 'Yes!'" Even though he was given the chassis, Mason purchased some of the spare components Kelly had stowed in his garage, such as steering and front wheels.

When Kelly originally purchased the dragster in the 1980s, he had been told it was built by renowned chassis designer Woody Gilmore. Once Mason took a good look at the chassis, he thought otherwise.

"The construction was fabulous, but it was so heavy," said Mason, who wondered why anyone would build a dragster that weighed so much.

Mason now owned an interesting car, but had no idea of its history. His search for information was starting from scratch. He hoped to restore the car, but first wanted to find out what he owned. He visited Don Garlits at his museum in Florida, but didn't get much insight from the famous Swamp Rat. He was having trouble authenticating the car. Admittedly, where he lived in the South, rail dragsters were rare and "door-slammers" were more popular.

One conclusion he came to was that because of the heavy weight and extra mounts welded to the chassis—even though Kelly had raced it

When nature called, Scott Mason walked behind buddy Karl Kelly's garage and discovered this old dragster chassis. Mason asked if he could have it and Kelly agreed. That started a several-year detective search to identify it. He finally realized he had one of the most popular twin-engined cars of the 1970s. *Scott Mason*

with one engine—the dragster was probably originally built to run with two engines.

"I bought every book I could find about front-engine dragsters and talked to everyone I could on the Internet," he said. "But I kept coming up empty."

Then a tip came out of the most unusual of places. Mason enjoys ballroom dancing, and during dance class one day another guy who knew that Mason was into cars approached him. "You know I build model cars," the man told Mason.

"I thought, Oh, God, here comes a story I don't want to hear," said Mason. "But actually he offered to post the photo of my dragster chassis on a drag racing website."

Mason received a call from a racing photographer.

"What you have there is not a Top Fuel car, but a Top Gas car," the caller said. "That's why it's built so heavy."

As a result, Mason sought out John Peters, the guru of multi-engine dragsters. "John led the multi-engine charge with his famous *Freight Train*, which ran two small-block Chevy engines," said Mason. "He told me the two-engine chassis were built extra stout because there was a lot of vibration with the

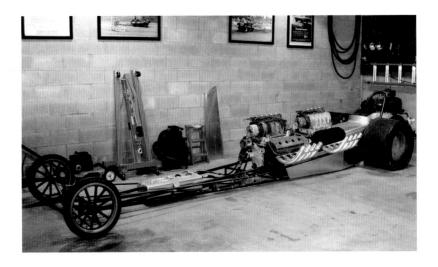

In this photo of the nearly restored dragster, Mason's hard work is obvious. He tracked down many of the original parts of the car from the shelves of the shop of the original builder. *Scott Mason*

multi-engine design. That problem was eventually solved when superchargers were added; the superchargers acted as balancing devices."

Mason was learning more and more about twin-engine dragsters in general, but not much more about his own chassis. That changed when he spoke with a couple of old-time racers.

"Funny Car driver Phil Elliott called and said, 'It appears that you own one of the sixty or seventy twin-engine cars that were built. A couple are still around.'"

Elliott suggested that Mason contact Hemi-engine builder Gene Adams, who looked at the photos and said, "I have no doubt that you have a twin-engine car. I suggest you call Shirley Muldowney and Bill Mullins, who both ran twin-engine cars."

"When he began thinking about running a multi-engine dragster, Mullins knew that Peters was running two small-block Chevy engines in his dragster, so he figured that if two small-blocks were good, two big-blocks would be better," said Mason. "So he built a dragster with two Hemi engines."

On Adam's recommendation, Mason tracked down drag racer Mullins, who in the late 1960s and early 1970s, decided to build a twin-engine car after he crashed his single-engine dragster at the Bristol, Tennessee, drag strip. Mason Googled Mullins and contacted him at Mullins Repair Service in Birmingham, Alabama.

Finally Mason was making progress; he believed the dragster in his garage was Mullins' old car. If so, it would have been built by Johnny Albright, who built a number of single-engine dragsters, but only one twin-engine car—the one for Mullins.

Mason sent photos of the car sitting in his garage to Mullins, who said, "That's my old car!"

Mason struck gold.

Mullins had raced the car nationally, and it was featured in *Hot Rod* magazine.

Mullins promised that he would begin looking for old parts for the dragster that might still be on the shelves at his shop. He discovered almost all the critical components for the dragster, including the all-important 5.86 rear axle.

"Mullins told me when you have two engines, you have more than twice the torque going to the pinion gear," said Mason. "It's easy to tear up the rear or destroy the clutch."

Having finally identified the car and its driver, Mason proceeded to have the car restored by both Mullins and J. Ed Horton of Belton, South Carolina. His requirement: restore the car back to the same specifications as when Mullins campaigned the car decades earlier.

"Rails have a rough life," said Mason. "Pieces get welded on and cut off with every engine change or every time the car changes hands."

Mason, who had by now owned the dragster for 10 years, loaded all the components he had collected into his truck and transported them down to Mullins' shop for a complete restoration.

"I asked him to restore it the way he thought it should done.

"Bill was the first Top Gas driver to break into the six-second bracket," said Mason. "This car is Bill's legacy."

40-Year Itch
Trans-Am Mustang

This 1965 Ford Mustang left the Ford assembly line as a plain Jane six-cylinder coupe, possibly driven out of the showroom by a librarian. But the life it went on to live was far from plain Jane.

Within a year, the Mustang had shed its six-cylinder engine for one of Ford's potent Hi-Po 289s, a four-speed, and a roll bar. Rather than commute to the library, the car regularly did battle on the Sports Car Club of America (SCCA) circuit.

Ray Heppenstall built the Mustang into a race car for amateur racer Buzz Marcus. Marcus entered the car in several SCCA A-Sedan races in 1966, including races held at Watkins Glen, New York, and Reading, Pennsylvania, winning three or four.

The Mustang had been modified with some hard-to-get parts. Instead of Mustang bucket seats, the coupe had black leather seats from a 289 Cobra. It also had a Cobra aluminum T-10 transmission and Carroll Shelby gauges.

Here Alderman comes in for a pit stop at the 1967 Sebring four-hour race, where he drove the full four hours solo because his co-driver, Unger, was unable to get leave from his military post to attend the race. Alderman finished ninth. *George Alderman collection*

Friends George Alderman and Brett Unger were itching to compete at Sebring in SCCA's new Trans-Am series for midsize sedans, but neither one of them owned a suitable car.

"Brett was in military service at the time, but thought he would be able to get off from time to time to race," said Alderman, now 77. "So we decided, 'let's go to Sebring!' So I called Buzz [Marcus] and we bought the car from him."

Alderman was a busy man, because around the same time, 1966, in Wilmington, Delaware, he opened

Forty-five years ago, veteran driver George Alderman campaigned anything on four wheels, including this 1965 Mustang Notchback, which he ran in the early Trans-Am series and co-owned with Brett Unger. The car had a Hi-Po 289 Engine, Cobra transmission, gauges, and seats. *George Alderman collection*

one of the first Datsun dealerships in the country, and a year later, he opened a Lotus franchise. In racing, Alderman drove everything from Formula Juniors to McLaren Can-Am cars during his long road racing career.

Maybe because he had raced so many British cars prior to the Mustang, he repainted the Caspian Blue coupe in British Racing Green. Alderman says that he believes the car still had a standard Hi-Po 289 with a single four-barrel carburetor that pulled cool air in from a modified cowl vent. In 1967, fuel cells were not required, so two Mustang gas tanks were split at the seams and the two larger sides were welded together, which gave it a much larger fuel capacity.

"Brett [Unger] couldn't get off for the Sebring races, so Bill Blankenship, who was working for me at the time, was signed on to be my co-driver at the Sebring four-hour Trans-Am race," said Alderman. "I came into the pits for fuel and a driver change, but Bill didn't even have his driver's suit on, so I just jumped back in and drove the rest of the race. I finished ninth." He also raced the car at Marlboro and Reading, but sold it to Norm Taylor in 1969.

Alderman went on to race additional races with Unger in a Lotus 23, then switched to Datsun 510s and Z-cars in IMSA, where he won the 1971 and 1974 Baby Grand Championships.

Alderman all but forgot about the old Mustang until 40 years later when his son, Paul, began racing and restoring old Mustangs. Taylor, who entered the car in a driver's school at Marlboro and street raced the Mustang, eventually

In January 2009, Alderman, his son Paul, and restoration friend Erich Bollman repurchased the car. They intend to restore it to its 1967 Trans-Am livery and begin vintage racing it. *George Alderman collection*

parked the tired old racer under a lean-to in the back lot of his commercial water business.

"I talked to Norm [Taylor] and his wife about twenty years ago to see if I could buy the car," said Paul Alderman. "I was told no and not to call again. But I knew one of their employees, and he told me the car was still there."

When Taylor died in the fall of 2008, a deal was agreed upon over a three-month period through a mutual friend, Bob Burris. But the deal nearly went awry.

"One of the Taylor's employees decided to clean up the storage yard after Norm died," said Paul. "There was a bunch of old trailers, an old Impala, and the Mustang. He decided to haul them all to the junkyard.

"We had to race to the junkyard to retrieve it before it got crushed. We never got to inspect the trailers, which we think had some of the original parts the car was missing, like the engine and the radiator."

But at least they had George's old race car back.

These days, the Aldermans own an automotive machine shop, having sold the Datsun/Nissan dealership several years ago. Certainly they can handle the rebuilding of the drivetrain, but restoration of the body, which had deteriorated badly, would require a pro. So the Aldermans made Erich Bollman, owner of Christiana Muscle Car Restoration, a partner in the car.

Paul and Erich hope to take turns racing the car in vintage sports car races when it is competed.

"It was such a neutral car to drive," said father George. "I was always right up there with the Corvettes when I raced it in A-Sedan."

A happy reunion, 40 years later.

The Junkyard Ferrari

By Rob Cotter

It was 1979, I was 23 and my sweetheart, Maureen, and I were taking time off to do the proverbial cross-country adventure that was so popular when a gallon of gas was one-quarter the price of a gallon milk.

I had recently restored an old Volvo 122 wagon for the trip. The car had a few mishaps during the 10,000-mile journey but came through when it mattered most. When Maureen rolled it several times down the steep passes of Yellowstone Park, both of us were unscathed from the accident. After several weeks of bending and welding, the Volvo was back on the road again. It just didn't look quite the same.

Although the old Volvo had flipped several times, it also bounced, so the passenger side looked like it was hit by a southbound train. Amazingly, the driver's side was perfect. We were roughly only halfway through our journey, and the car's condition led to numerous conversations along the way. (I was tempted to write "His" and "Hers" on each side of the car, but that would've made for a long, cold trip.)

In Arcata, California, the heart of redwood country, we had one of our weekly breakdowns. It was the usual routine. We'd visit friends and locate the appropriate auto parts store, and then I'd spend the remainder of our visit on my back on our friend's driveway.

I was pulling into downtown Arcata when I noticed quite a unique vehicle; a mid-1960s Comber camper van. At the time it was probably the only one I'd ever seen, sort of a British version of a VW Camper. I looked it over and was amazed it was still on the road and running. I went into the parts store, but when I came back outside, a fellow was staring at my Volvo just as intently. It was the guy who owned the Comber. He wanted to know if I needed any Volvo parts and instructed me to follow him and the Comber back to his place.

I remember lots of twisting roads up steep hills. That Comber was the slowest vehicle imaginable, desperately sputtering and straining to go even five miles per hour. It made my old, demolished 122 wagon seem like a Turbo Carrera as I slowly crawled behind him. After about 20 minutes of driving we arrived at his house/junkyard/laboratory, only two miles away from where we started.

My first impression was that it appeared to be a typical foreign car junkyard from the mid-1960s, only decades later. The lot contained Peugeots, Morris Minors, Humbers, Alfa Romeos—the list went on. But there were some distinctly unique aspects to the atmosphere of this salvage yard. One was the music (don't all junkyards have piped-in music as the customers rummage

The beat-up remains of a once great racer. This rare 340/375 MM Ferrari, which had been raced by famous drivers such as Phil Hill, Carroll Shelby, Richie Ginther, and Alberto Ascari, as well as Lou Brero Sr., sat in a storage container in a California junkyard for 40 years. *Mark Savory*

through rusted Citroëns?). The classical music was performed by a group called the "Harmonicats," which is an all-harmonica band. During my time in Arcata, the music was always on and the Harmonicats were the only thing playing. My other impression was of his office, which was housed inside a 1930s stream-lined bus. The office was decorated with rows of purple velvet drapes with gold cherubs hung from the walls every six feet or so. As strange as this all was, the office and music was pretty mundane compared with the automotive oddities that rested on these hallowed grounds.

The scruffy-looking junkyard owner introduced himself as Lou Brero Jr. He seemed nice enough, as well as exceedingly eccentric. He mentioned he was going through a rough divorce.

We became car friends, and he shared some of his life experiences with me and showed me some of his inventions. There was the 4WD Morris Minor pickup truck with the Porsche 356 motor mounted to a dual-range eight-speed gearbox and the Bultaco motorcycle with the Honda engine and the strange sidecar that doubled as a canoe and hot air balloon gondola.

The streamlined bus/office with purple curtains and gold cherubs was being restored and highly modified to maintain 100-mile-per-hour speeds. The back of the bus was being fitted with a drop-down tailgate that would serve as a garage for the Porsche-powered Morris. This was all in preparation for an around-the-world trip of a lifetime, and I got the impression he was waiting for some sort of financial settlement to begin his trip.

As we extracted parts from the old collection of Volvos (I needed a lot!), I learned a bit about his personality, which could benevolently have been described as peculiar, if not cause for concern. At one point I had gotten some rusted car crud in my eyes, and Lou saw I had to stop and deal with the irritation. "Oh, let me show you how to deal with this," he said, at which point he grabbed a handful of dirt and tossed it into his open eyes. Then he grabbed a file and aggressively started grinding away at his knuckles until they bled. "Then you wipe dirt and grease into the cuts, and NOW you are ready to work on a car!" He did all of this to the tune of Beethoven's Fifth being played by Mighty Mouse.

I began to get seriously concerned about spending time with this man. But the thought of continuing driving the 122 with a rear shock bouncing though the floorboard was worth the risk of dealing with this, um, frustrated artist.

Sometimes I would get to the yard and he would be dealing with other issues, and I would mill about through the glorious rubble. As I'm kicking about between the cut-in-half English taxicabs and the bombed-out Sunbeam Rapiers, I spy a unique engine block. It was a V-12!

Quickly my mind started racing. "How many brands of V-12s are there even out there?" The heads were stripped off and the cylinders looked smallish. Wait, there were more. Two more V-12 blocks outside under old vinyl tablecloths! WOW! What a discovery. Now my goal was not only to get the Volvo parts for my ailing wagon, but to purchase from this crazy man these V-12 blocks and the magnificent piece of iron that hopefully went with them.

Lou returned to give his attention to me. It turns out he was chasing cats on the property with a tire iron. "Filthy, murderous bastards! They kill for pleasure. I hate them and won't have them around me," he said. Now I'm scared again.

As he was hauling out a cutting torch to dismember a donor Volvo I timidly asked, "Hey Lou, I noticed a V-12 block over there under the tarp?"—only mentioning one in hopes that he's too distracted even to remember about the other two. "Yeah, that's to my '53 Ferrari," he mentions matter-of-factly.

I stammer, "F-F-Fifty-Three F-F-Ferrari?"

"Yeah, it's a 1953, the one my father raced at the Nassau races."

I'm sure he could hear my jaw drop when it hit the ground. This led to a whole other unique chapter in this man's life. Yes, his father was a Ferrari racer and had one of the earliest Ferraris in the United States. But Lou himself raced for Alfa Romeo in Italy. He went into great detail as to being the outcast of the team, the "Young American Rebel." Alfa management had little patience for his radical style. I seemed to remember him telling me that one of their gripes was that he would spin his wheels too much on the turns. He thought it would

Fully restored and now owned by collector Bruce McCaw, the "Junkyard Ferrari" won Best of Show, Concours de Sport, at the 2007 Amelia Island Concours d'Elegance. *Neil Rashba*

orient his car better in the turns, but they just thought he was a showboat. And I think there was also alcohol involved.

Eventually, he said, Alfa management worked with the Italian police to have him removed from the country, thus ending his international racing career.

Closer to home, he once raced an outdated Kurtis sports car that famously beat the Corvette factory team.

Anyway, I was still starstruck with the notion of leaving with a 1953 Ferrari. "Hey Lou, how much do you want for the old Ferrari anyway?" He dryly responded, "I want one million dollars." I almost fell over. Bear in mind, this is back when a million dollars was like . . . a MILLION DOLLARS! My heart sank. I guess he wasn't that crazy. But at least I needed to see it before I left.

He pointed out where it was. A dozen yards away was a series of old storage containers where cars and other items were stored. Overstuffed doesn't begin to describe how tightly these containers were packed. Collectively the units held about 12 cars in them. Cars were literally stacked on top of each other. Inside was a Hudson, a Packard, picnic tables standing on end, swing sets, an aluminum rowboat (powered by an inboard 305 Honda Dream motorcycle engine, with some sort of jet-drive installed, of course). And way in the back of one unit, peeking out from all that shit, was the edge of a left front fender, headlight, and the corner of a grille of a 1940s Ferrari. Underneath mounds of dust and gunk, it almost looked red. It was like getting a glimpse of a starlet from afar that you could never embrace—nor would anyone else—for a couple of decades.

This was the same car—375 MM serial number 286 AM—that won the Nürburgring 1000 in 1953, and the next year Phil Hill and Richie Ginther used the car to finish second in the Carrera Panamerican.

I occasionally think of that strange junkyard with the numerous contraptions, but only one popped back on the radar. In the 1990s, a group of wealthy investors and Ferrari collectors rescued the Ferrari and paid the required ransom, overpriced but a worthy cause. For me, I felt grateful to get out of there in one piece and with enough Volvo parts to continue our journey. I wonder if anyone knows about an all-wheel-drive Porsche-powered Morris out there?

And I wonder if Lou ever took that around-the-world extravaganza in his streamliner?

I hope so.

Update

It has been nearly 40 years since Lou Brero's famous 1953 Ferrari 340 MM Vignale Spyder RHD with the oversized 375 engine was last seen in public. In its early days, it came in first at Nürburgring piloted by Alberto Ascari and Giuseppe Farina. Later it ran in the Pan Americana with Luigi Chinetti and accumulated numerous first and seconds with Phil Hill, Caroll Shelby, and Lou Brero Sr. It was later sold by Lou Brero Jr. for $1.5 million, complete with an interior filled with cedar chips and a partially installed Jaguar drivetrain. But the car was complete and intact though well-rusted and in pieces.

Just weeks later it sold again to Bruce McCaw of Bellevue, Washington, for $1.8 million and was immediately sent for restoration to Pete Lovely Racing. In 1997, it debuted at the Monterey Historic Automobile Races. With Phil Hill at the wheel, it won by lapping the entire field. It has since won the Pebble Beach Cup at the 1997 Pebble Beach Concours d'Elegance and the Concours d'Competicione at Amelia Island in 2007.

CHAPTER 7

Reunited

The Snake and
the Satellite

Most adult males between the ages of 35 and 55 will remember the Mongoose and the Snake. These were aliases for two Funny Car drivers, Tom "Mongoose" McEwen and Don "Snake" Prudhomme, whose rivalry was made famous by Mattel Hot Wheels. Mattel manufactured scale versions of the two drag race cars, and millions of American boys had these cars in their toy collections in the 1960s and 1970s.

Prudhomme and McEwen raced against each other from coast-to-coast for years, all the while their performances being advertised and marketed by Mattel to young boys.

The program eventually ended, and the two drivers went on to other sponsorships. Nearly 40 years later, even men who have become successful CEOs of major corporations will crack a smile when the Mongoose and the Snake are mentioned.

The two men have retired from driving drag race cars, but both are still very involved in the sport. McEwen is associate publisher of *Drag Racer* magazine, and Prudhomme owns a Top Fuel drag racing team. And both still look back fondly on their days as one of drag racing's most durable rivalries.

Several years ago, Prudhomme began to search for and purchase his old drag race cars for a personal museum he established at his headquarters in Vista, California. So far he has discovered and restored his Hot Wheels Barracuda, U.S. Army Plymouth Arrow, Pepsi Challenger Trans-Am Pontiac, and the U.S. Army Vega.

In addition to his old drag cars, Prudhomme wanted to buy back his old Dodge D-700 race car transporter that he had driven to drag strips from one end of the country to the other earlier in his career.

The truck has quite an interesting history, as Prudhomme explains:

"Back in the day, Plymouth was involved with Richard Petty, and his Hemi NASCAR teams used to barnstorm around the country, sometimes racing two or three times a week. Plymouth had Dodge build Petty this truck with a special crew cab.

"When McEwen and I got together with the Hot Wheels program, we wanted to have some fancy trucks to haul our race cars around. Other drag racing teams—Sox & Martin and Dick Landy—had these bitchin' crew cab Dodges too, and we thought we should have some trucks just like those."

Prudhomme heard through Chrysler executive, Dick Maxwell, that Petty had just traded his two-year-old truck into a Greensboro, North Carolina, dealership.

"I bought the 1967 truck from that dealership in 1969 for a couple of thousand dollars, which was a lot of money for me back then," he said. "Dodge didn't make many of those crew cab bodies. The rear doors are actually front doors that are cut down and modified. NASCAR wanted the crew cab bodies so they could haul their teams around to the tracks. Not too many other people needed a body like that."

Immediately after purchasing the truck, Prudhomme brought the truck to Nash Enterprises in California and had a custom body built to haul the Funny Car. The body featured a 50-gallon fuel tank, cabinets, tire racks, and an engine cabinet.

Hall of Fame drag racer Don Prudhomme, the Snake, sought to find, purchase, and restore the old hauler he had used for years to transport his drag cars to strips around the country. Using an old VIN number, a police friend, and Google Earth, he was able to identify the Dodge hauler in a Southern California backyard! *Don Prudhomme collection*

McEwen bought a similar truck and had a similar custom rear body fabricated.

"I used this truck through our Hot Wheels program—1969, 1970, 1971, 1972, and sold it in 1973," said Prudhomme. "I sold it, but years later I started to buy and restore a lot of my old cars, but this truck was always in the back of my mind. It was featured in that movie narrated by Paul Newman called *Once Upon a Wheel*, where it featured the second Hot Wheels paint job.

"I sold it to a guy out in the [San Fernando] Valley back in the '70s, and I started to think that maybe I could find it again."

While going through some old paperwork and records, Prudhomme's wife, Lynn, found the original bill of sale. She said to her husband, "Wow, here's the original receipt and the VIN from the truck!"

Prudhomme took the VIN number to a law enforcement friend of his, and they began to search for the truck.

"We found out that it was last registered in 1996," he said, "just over twenty years after I sold it.

"So we found the address and began to do a MapQuest search."

Prudhomme figured that it would be too large to fit in a garage.

"We got on the Google Earth program on our computer and searched for the guy's address," he said. "We looked right at this house in the middle of Pocoima, and, zip, right there in the backyard was my truck!

Because Prudhomme couldn't find anyone with a shop big enough to work on the truck, he and his crew restored the truck themselves back to its Hot Wheels livery. Here he is standing next to his just-finished restoration, his first big-time racing rig. *Don Prudhomme collection*

"That's my truck!"

Prudhomme could tell it was his truck, even though there was an old junk car on the back.

"So I asked a friend of mine who is a cop who works out of San Fernando to go to this address and check out the truck," said Prudhomme. "He called me back after he peeked over the fence and said, 'If it's a crew cab,' and he gave me some details, 'it's your old truck.'"

Prudhomme called the current owner of the truck, who knew that it once belonged to the drag racing legend, and said he was interested in buying the truck back. The good news is that the owner had thought about selling the truck; the bad news is that he wanted to put it on eBay. Prudhomme attempted to purchase the truck directly from the owner, without risking an inflated price through eBay.

"So I asked him how much he wanted for the truck," continued Prudhomme. "He told me fifty thousand dollars.

"Fifty grand? I told him good luck.

"So the guy said, 'Make me an offer.' I told him ten thousand dollars."

Prudhomme reminds us that he hadn't even seen the truck in person, except from the satellite photos from miles up in space.

"But I figured anything has to be worth that much," he said. "The guy kept telling me how bitchin' the truck was, so as we drove up there I'm thinking that my old truck is in great shape. This was ideal, because I really didn't want to do a lot of work on it—just a quick paint job."

Before he left to pick up the truck, he contacted a paint shop to tell them he'd be dropping off his old truck for a new Hot Wheels yellow paint job.

"So we pull up in front of this guy's house in Pocoima, and I say, 'That can't be my truck!'" said Prudhomme. "It had a big, ugly, old bumper in the front, and the guy was standing up on the hood and some kid was inside the cab.

"Inside it was all rotted out, with crap all over the seats. He was trying to start the truck using a glass container for a fuel tank.

"I said to the guy, 'Are you shitting me?' I was so pumped up to buy the truck, but it was such a piece of junk. They had cut up the body to make it easier to haul around junk cars. The body was all rotted from sitting outside its whole life.

"I told the guy I didn't even want the truck. Then the guy got pissed at me, so I just left."

But before Prudhomme pulled the plug on the whole deal, he called his friend and former crew chief Neil Armstrong for advice. He reminded Prudhomme that the rusted truck was the only crew cab example remaining of that type of transporter.

"So I called the truck owner back and said I'd take it," he said. "I wound up paying a little more than ten thousand dollars for it."

Prudhomme sent a huge wrecker to retrieve the retired hauler. The truck took a long time to restore, because virtually every piece was worn-out or rusted. He said that all the undercarriage hardware, including king pins, springs, steering components, and brakes, needed to be replaced before the truck could be moved around.

Even though the truck had lots of rust, both the truck body and the rear utility body are original. Prudhomme decided to give the project to a shop to handle the restoration.

"We found this guy with a huge shop who could sandblast the entire body inside a room," said Prudhomme. "It's so hard to find someone who can sandblast something that big. So this guy is sandblasting and beginning to do bodywork when his company goes bankrupt.

"So we just took the project over and completed it in our shop. It took a couple of years to complete. We kept it original with power steering and power brakes, but it didn't have air conditioning then, and it doesn't have air conditioning now. But it does have air brakes, which work great."

This truck is now the crown jewel in Prudhomme's impressive collection. It has been restored to a Pebble Beach Concours quality. Instead of having an employee drive this rig, Prudhomme mostly drives this one himself. For old time's sake, in October, 2009, he left his shop near San Diego, picked up his old friend and teammate Tom McEwen in Orange, California, and drove it to the annual Hot Rod Reunion in Bakersfield, where it was a hit with the fans.

Prudhomme admits that Google Earth helped him repurchase his old set of wheels, but he warns, "You better be careful with those satellites overhead, because they'll catch you if you're picking your nose in your backyard."

The Cornfield
Hemi 'Cuda

G reg Peterson drove a yellow Corvair Spyder convertible during his high school years. He graduated with honors, and his proud father and grandfather wanted to send Greg off to engineering school driving a brand-new car.

Greg didn't mind his Corvair, which handled well and was reliable, but both his dad and granddad were car enthusiasts. They wanted to reward him for doing so well in school with something a little sportier.

Greg was given a choice of either a new Corvette or a Plymouth Hemi 'Cuda. In 1970, the 17-year-old, his father, and his grandfather walked into Carlson Motor Sales in Morris, Illinois, to order the 'Cuda. The son may have been reluctant to give up his Corvair, but his father was more than prepared to place the order for him. Mr. Peterson had studied the sales brochure well,

How many times have you driven past a farm and wondered what was sitting behind the barn doors? Ninety-nine percent of the time it's just an old tractor or a pickup truck at best. But this particular barn near Morris, Illinois, had a special vehicle inside, and, yup, it was powered by a Hemi. *Scott Smith*

Greg Peterson (pictured) pulls open the door to reveal what is possibly the best original Hemi 'Cuda in the world, the 1971 'Cuda he received for achieving good grades in high school 40 years earlier. *Scott Smith*

Carefully wrapped up with a car cover and a plastic sheet underneath, Peterson preserved his 11,000-mile 426 Hemi-powered 'Cuda on the family farm since it was last driven in 1974. *Scott Smith*

and when they sat down with the salesman, he rattled off the list of options he desired: a 426 Hemi engine, four-speed transmission, Trac-Pac 3:54 Dana 60 rear end, TorRed paint, black leather bucket seats, power steering, power brakes, power windows, 15x7-inch Rallye Wheels, AM/FM radio with rear speaker, Rallye dash gauges, three-spoke wood steering wheel, dual-painted Sport Mirrors, painted grille, and rear window defroster.

The salesman calculated a retail price, but the three shrewd farmers sitting in front of him haggled fiercely. When a fair price was agreed upon, the salesman told them that he dropped the price only because he always wanted to sell a Hemi car.

On January 30, 1971, Greg received a call that his new car had arrived and it was ready to be picked up. Once he drove it home, he realized two things about his new car: one was that it was a handful to drive compared to his Corvair; and the other was that fender lip moldings were only installed in the driver's side of the 'Cuda. That was curious, because he had not even ordered fender moldings. The embarrassed dealer couldn't explain the mishap. He installed the same moldings on the passenger side and sent young Greg down the road, but not before giving him a small paper packet of special valve stem extensions that were required with the Rallye Wheels. Greg installed those extensions when he

A real time capsule and 100 percent authentic right down to the original spark plugs. *Scott Smith*

got home and saved the original short extensions in the packet and placed it inside the center console.

Greg didn't really enjoy driving his new car. He found it irritating that it was hard to take off from a stop sign without spinning the rear tires. His high school yearbook had a photo of Greg and his 'Cuda with a handwritten sign in the rear window that read "Chevy Eater," but he was no speed demon. During his high school and college years, he never received a speeding ticket, had an accident, or even had a flat tire.

Preferring his Corvair's less aggressive nature, Greg drove the 'Cuda sparingly, accumulating only 11,318 miles before parking it in his family's barn in 1974.

Fastforward more than three decades: During the summer of 2006, Scott Smith was surfing the web when he came across a post that someone wanted to get his 'Cuda's carburetors rebuilt. Smith, who restores Mopar muscle cars and rebuilds components, responded with an email but didn't think much more about it.

The next day, Smith received a phone call from the gentleman who posted the request. "He told me the carbs were for his '71 Hemi 'Cuda, which didn't

The 'Cuda's first trip outdoors since 1974, the virgin 'Cuda looks and runs like a brand-new car. Besides the 426 Hemi and four-speed, the car was ordered with a number of unusual options at the time, such as power windows, wood spoke steering wheel, and AM/FM radio. *Scott Smith*

The original tires, including the valve stem extensions, still hold 1974 air! *Scott Smith*

surprise me too much because of all the clones out there," said Smith.

"I asked him if the carburetors were complete, and the caller said yes, that they had only eleven thousand miles on them. He said he hadn't started the car since 1974."

The phone call was, of course, from Greg Petersen. He wanted to refresh the car that had been sitting in the barn since the mid-1970s.

"Greg told me his barber, who had a generic

Interestingly, Peterson still owns the Corvair convertible he drove in high school before receiving the 'Cuda. It is also parked in the barn. He was uncomfortable driving the 'Cuda because the wheels would break loose too easily. *Scott Smith*

photo of a Hemi 'Cuda hanging on the wall in his shop, one day mentioned to him, 'Too bad you still don't have your old 'Cuda,' to which Greg answered, 'Yes I do.' Then the barber said, 'Oh, it probably needs a lot of restoration,' to which Greg responded, 'No, it's just like I parked it.'"

Greg had also seen the televised Barrett-Jackson Auction and saw a similar car to his sell for about $1 million.

"He told me he bought it new, but parked it after driving it after just a few years," said Smith. "I asked him to please not do anything to the car because I wanted to see it with my own eyes before any work was done."

Travel arrangements were quickly made, and soon Smith was on a flight from Washington to Chicago to document this very rare survivor.

When Smith arrived in Chicago, he had no idea what to expect. Was the story real? Was it a clone? As he pulled his rental car up to the storage barn in the middle of a cornfield, he expected to see a tractor or some other farm implement inside. Instead, he faced the most original 1971 Hemi 'Cuda on the planet, a time capsule that had not seen the light of day in 33 years.

"The car had been parked on a packed gravel and dirt floor," said Smith. "After all the years, the tires, which still had 1974 air in them, had sunken about one inch into the ground. We pushed it outside and gave it a gentle sponge bath. Then I photographed the heck out of it."

Peterson had never washed under the hood, so all the original markings and details were still intact.

Smith was treated to a virgin example of a Hemi 'Cuda: the undercarriage was untouched and no replacement parts had ever been installed; the interior had no noticeable wear, and the carpet and wooden steering wheel still looked

Open wide and say . . . vroom! This time-capsule Hemi 'Cuda hadn't seen daylight since 1974, nearly 32 years. According to Scott Smith, who authenticated the car, it is perhaps the most original Hemi 'Cuda in existence. *Scott Smith photo*

like brand-new; the paint, although it had a few parking lot scuffs, still shone like new; the chrome bumpers and other bright trim was still bright; all the glass was scratch free; and the argent paint on the shaker bubble still had the original deep luster.

"Greg admitted that he was no mechanic, and never lifted the hood other than to check the oil," said Smith, who was pleased to see the carburetors still had the plastic limiter caps on the adjusting screws.

"Greg requested that all the parts [that] dealership mechanics removed from the car during tune-ups be returned. So he had the original spark plugs. The only items that were not original to the car when it came off the assembly line was the oil filter, battery, negative battery cable, and a short piece of three-eighths-inch fuel line that had begun to deteriorate."

Apparently the 'Cuda was so powerful that Peterson said he regularly consumed Rolaids to help calm his stomach. Inside the center console, Smith discovered a half-consumed package of Rolaids! Oh, and remember the small packet of tire valve extensions? Those were also still in the console too.

Smith returned home but made plans to return to help Peterson get the 'Cuda running.

"On my next visit, in the spring of 2007, I told Greg I felt like I was entering King Tut's tomb," said Smith. "I wanted to get the car running, but didn't want to destroy the originality, like by removing the gas tank.

"I disconnected the fuel line and pulled the distributor out to prime the oil pump. I bungee-corded a one-gallon fuel can to the firewall, and the engine fired right up. It was a beautiful thing, and it didn't even smoke."

Peterson and Smith drove the car down the street and into the driveway of the Peterson house where the car was parked everyday in the 1970s.

Since that time, Peterson has asked Smith to assist him in selling the car to a collector. Smith says that at a market high several years ago, the car probably had a value of $1 million, but the current economy has brought the value down to between $600,000 and $700,000.

"We notified some of the big players in the Mopar collecting world, but didn't get any real bites," said Smith. "Then we put the car on eBay, and got an offer of eight hundred forty-nine thousand dollars, but the purchaser was a fraud. Today we're hoping to find someone who wants to own the best, most original Hemi on the planet.

"I can't imagine a Holier Grail."

The Back-to-School Roadster

By John Lee

Fifty years ago, no one in the little Kansas prairie town that Ron Kester calls home paid much attention to whether or not a kid driving down the street had a driver's license. Most of them grew up on farms and learned to drive tractors, combines, farm trucks, or the family sedan at an early age. Unless they were acting up or overly reckless, probably neither one of the two local cops would get his shorts in a bunch seeing a young buck behind the steering wheel of an old car, as long as he could see over the steering wheel.

When he was 13 years old, Ron had an after-school and weekend job sweeping floors and doing odd jobs at the local implement dealer. An old 1930 Model A Ford coupe sat out in the weather behind the place. When Ron got his paycheck one fall Friday in 1954, he finally had saved the $35.00 it would take to buy it, and he did.

He drove the coupe home and the same afternoon, with the help of some friends, flipped the deck lid over to make it a rumble seat and cut the roof off to make a roadster. "We had it in the homecoming parade that night," Ron related, "but only made it halfway. A fuel line plugged up, so we had to push it to the end of the parade route." Fortunately, Phillipsburg, Kansas, is a very small town.

The next day the fenders and running boards came off to give the former coupe more of a hot rod look, further distinguished by retaining the full door frames. Ron said the only cushion in the rumble seat was a pile of blankets, but none of the high-schoolers who were regular passengers complained.

Inspecting the Model A closely, a piece of pipe can be seen sticking up about six inches above the body line just behind the middle of the seat. That was to wrap the rope around when you wanted to give some friends a thrill ride on an upside-down car hood on a snow-covered country road or frozen lake.

The Model A provided on- and off-the-road transportation for Ron and several friends during their high school years. Keeping it running and making modifications on a whim laid the foundation for Ron's future automotive endeavors. As he moved on to other things, he said, "I never had any idea where that old Model A went."

Among a parade of interesting cars that followed was the one he probably envisioned when he bought the Model A at age 13—a sweet 1932 Ford five-window coupe street rod.

This rusty relic of a Model A Ford coupe didn't attract too much attention in the junkyard because of its terrible condition, except to Ron Kester. He realized it was the very hot rod he had built when he was in high school 50 years earlier. Luckily he was able to repurchase it. *John Lee*

After several years of honing his mechanical and body modification skills on his own rides, Ron turned his hobby into a business. Ron's Restoration celebrated its 20th anniversary in business in 2009. It's the largest business in Glade, Kansas, a tiny town seven miles from Phillipsburg. The shop has turned out a long string of award-winning restorations, street rods, and customs.

Some 40 years after he last saw his first car, Ron got a call. A fellow by the

Kester (pictured) has since restored the car to the same condition as when he drove it in high school. He did make one deviation, though; he installed a hopped-up flathead Ford V-8 instead of the four-cylinder engine it once had.
John Lee

name of Art Ehm had passed away. Art had run a salvage yard of sorts a few miles west of Phillipsburg; let's just say it had never won a Business of the Year award. There were 47 old cars on the property, and Ehm's heirs asked Ron to give them an idea of what the accumulation was worth. He ended up buying the whole lot, the best of which was a restorable 1958 Ford convertible and accompanying parts car.

Ron, his brother, and some employees spent several weeks of their spare

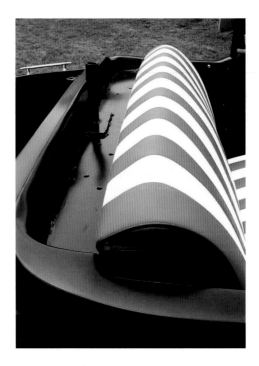

Look carefully, and behind the striped seat you'll see a vertical pole that Kester used to tow sledders during snowstorms in his youth. This is how he was able to positively identify his old rod.
John Lee

time going though the stash, hauling a few of the cars with restoration potential back to the shop, stripping usable parts, and sending the remaining hulks to the crusher. They about had the junk lot cleared when one of the salvage crew called, "Hey, Ron, take a look at this!"

"We went over to check out a plum thicket," he related, "and uncovered my old Model A! It was so covered up we hadn't even known there was anything there. I had no idea the car had been there all these years, just a few miles away."

The cut-off coupe-turned-roadster still bore the bent frame horns where he had hit a cedar tree. "I still had the bent bumper and the steering wheel that I'd kept all those years," he said. The car also had all four 16-inch wire wheels and hubcaps Ron had put on it. The four-cylinder engine was frozen tight.

They loaded up the Model A and hauled it to a spot behind the shop, where it would spend another few years before the right time arrived to put it back on the street.

"I decided I wanted to get it ready for my fifty-year class reunion on Memorial Day weekend 2009," said Ron. "We worked on it nights and weekends for a year."

The chassis was assembled from spare parts they found around the shop—1940 Ford hydraulic brakes, a 1951 Ford pickup master cylinder, hydraulic shocks, etc. The 16-inch wires were painted red and fitted with bias-ply wide whitewalls and trim rings. The body and frame were restored to probably the best condition of their long life and finished with black primer. Sealed-beam headlights, 1946 Chevrolet taillights, and one of Ron's specially machined propeller radiator caps were among the finishing touches. The rumble seat had a cushion finally and red and white candy stripe vinyl upholstery to match the front seat.

The car had never gotten as far as the Model A V-8 hot rod Ron may have first envisioned in the 1950s, but that has now been remedied. He bought a 1946 AB 24-stud flathead from his Northwest Kansas rodding buddy Darrel Wark and built it up with Speedway Motors' repro Edelbrock high-compression heads, fuel lines and fuel block, water pumps, air cleaners, headers, and Smitty mufflers. Twin Ford Holley 94 carbs ride atop an Offenhauser intake.

It's not often that someone gets to drive to his 50-year class reunion in the very car he drove in high school. But thanks to a lucky find in a plum thicket, together with some highly developed restoration skills and a well-equipped shop, Ron Kester has managed to return to the 1950s in cool, hot rod style!

Honest Mike's
Lucky Day

They call him Honest Mike. He worked for a guy named Honest Charlie, who ran one of the country's premier speed shops through the 1960s and 1970s. Mike was Charlie's right-hand man.

When Charlie passed away and the company closed, Mike Goodman worked for other hot rod parts suppliers, but he always dreamed of the day he could reopen the speed shop that used some of the most unique marketing in the industry to sell hot rod parts.

That day came when fellow Chattanooga businessman, Corky Coker, head of Coker Tire Company, approached Goodman about reestablishing the brand and reopening up the shop.

Goodman chomped at the bit and Honest Charlie's was again in operation.

Part of the marketing plan meant that Mike was required to man a mobile marketing unit that was used to sell hot rod parts at major car shows around the United States.

He loved it.

As he sold T-shirts, dropped front axles, and headlights for old Fords, he met folks who had grown up buying parts from Honest Charlie decades earlier. They told Goodman stories, and he loved hearing them. In fact, talking to customers became the highlight of his weekends.

One day in 2004 at AutoFair at Lowe's Motor Speedway, he was selling T-shirts when he heard a voice behind him. Selling parts and talking to a guy behind him was no problem for Goodman, a famous multitasker.

"Know anyone who wants to buy an old Ford?" said the mystery voice behind him.

"What kind of old Ford?" Goodman asked without turning around.

"An old Ford coupe," said the voice.

"What kind?" asked Goodman, still not turning around.

"A 1932 five-window," said the voice.

"How long have you owned it?" Goodman asked.

"I've owned it since 1959, but my uncle bought it in 1934," said the mystery voice. "It was my high school hot rod."

The voice got Goodman's attention. He turned around.

"How much?" asked Goodman, still facing his T-shirt customer.

When the man told him, Goodman wanted to know where the car was.

Mike Goodman (pictured), of Honest Charlie's Speed Shop, became the owner of this very authentic 1932 Ford "Deuce" five-window coupe just because he's a nice guy. The previous owner saw how much fun Goodman was having with customers at his parts booth and asked him, "Know anyone who wants to buy an old Ford?" *Mike Goodman collection*

"It's in my brother's barn, but we can drive it out," the man said.

"When I finished selling the T-shirt, I turned around again and he was gone," Goodman said.

"My heart stopped."

But thankfully the man, Archie Hinton, returned later and spoke about the car's location, which was in Ohio.

Goodman and his colleague, Dolas Ferguson, were driving from Chattanooga, Tennessee, to Carlisle, Pennsylvania, for the big swap meet when they detoured to visit the man in Belpre, Ohio.

"Dolas and I just knew the car would turn out to be a fiberglass Model A," said Goodman.

It was raining as the two pulled their truck in front of the Hintons' house and planned their approach.

"We were going to act real cool," he said, "but there it was, sitting in the mist, just idling away."

"I was so excited, I was ready to bounce off the walls."

Goodman and Ferguson walked into the Hintons' house, which was jam-packed with racing artifacts. It was obvious that he was well-connected in both the antique car and racing worlds.

"Why didn't you sell this car to a local?" asked Goodman, realizing that Hinton didn't have to come all the way to Charlotte to sell a car he could have sold near his hometown.

"My wife hates this car, and my kids don't appreciate it," said Hinton. "And my friends were all trying to beat me out of it."

Hinton reminisced about his early days with the coupe when his wife joined into the conversation.

"We went on our first date in it," she said. "But I didn't like the heat coming off the floor then, and I don't like it now.

"I hate the car."

They went back outside and gave the car a good inspection. It had a 21-stud, 1934 Ford flathead engine with a two-barrel carburetor. It had a strange combination of having hydraulic brakes in the back and mechanical brakes in the front.

The car rolled on 16-inch wire wheels.

"The car was maroon with black fenders," said Goodman. "It was just like a '32 hot rod you would have owned in 1959."

Goodman questioned his good fortune; why had Hinton chosen him as the next owner of such a desirable car?

"Hinton said that when he walked up to our booth in Charlotte, I was having a good time and knew I was the kind of guy who would enjoy the car."

Goodman bought the car, loaded it in the trailer, and left for Carlisle for the swap meet, where Honest Charlie's had a booth. They unloaded the car and had it sit in front of the booth to attract attention. He hadn't noticed that his partner, Coker—a famous practical joker—had put a for sale sign on the windshield.

"A guy came up to me and says he's going to buy my car," said Goodman. "I told him, 'No, you're not; it's not for sale.' He said, 'Yes, it is,' and I said, 'No, it's not.'"

Goodman then noticed Coker and his staff doubled over in laughter, and it was then he saw the for sale sign posted on it.

Once Goodman got the car home, he jacked it up and crawled underneath. It was definitely a teenager's hot rod.

"You could see that Hinton wanted to lower the car, so they sagged the springs with a three-hundred-pound piece of steel that was bolted onto the floor," he said.

"This car represents a piece of American hot rod history, like a time capsule.

"Hinton was a sincere guy, and he saw that I was as well, and sincere car people attract sincere car people."

Striking Carerra Gold

Most collectors feel great about finding an undiscovered classic that's been hidden for decades. Sometimes, though, just finding an interesting part of a classic is enough.

Jim Kane ran into a guy who had purchased an interesting collection of cars from a towing company storage yard. He told Kane that many towing companies advertise "We Buy Junk Cars."

"Hmmm," Kane, 50, thought, "Maybe other towing companies have cars available as well. . . ."

Kane is a lifelong car enthusiast who has an interest in classics built in 1918 as well as 1970s muscle cars.

So in the spring of 2009 he was off, stopping first at the Collin's Tow Yard near his Indianapolis home. They had a 1967 Chevy Malibu convertible and a 1957 Porsche coupe available. "Why would a towing company have an old Porsche?" he thought as he purchased the two cars.

The Porsche was rough; it had an engine where the back seat belonged and had no seats or engine cover.

"The guy at the towing company told me a few more parts might still be available for the Porsche from the guy who had owned it since the 1960s," he said.

"He said extra parts might still be stored inside the leaky storage shed where the Porsche had been parked for so many years," said Kane. "That would explain the rust on the car."

Kane found out that the Porsche was owned by Jake Smith, and the Chevy was owned by his wife. The two cars had been parked for many years inside a storage shed in anticipation of one day being restored. When the Smiths came to the realization that their dream cars had deteriorated too far to be restored, they called Collins Towing, who advertised that they purchased junk cars.

The towing operator said one more thing that got Kane's attention. "Jake also has a Carrera engine available."

"I told him I was interested," said Kane, who sought more information on how a rare four-cam Carrera engine had become separated from its car. Once he spoke personally to the owner, the pieces started to come together.

"Back in the 1960s, the owner of a Porsche Carrera Speedster, VIN A3260, threw a connecting rod and needed an engine," said Kane. "He brought the car to the local Porsche specialist, Sam Mustard, who removed the four-cam Carrera engine [No. 90785] from the Speedster and installed a 1,600cc pushrod engine."

Jim Kane of Indianapolis bought a rusty Porsche 356 from a local towing company, but followed a lead that led him to this very rare four-cam Porsche Carrera engine. He is storing the engine in his spare bedroom. *Jim Kane*

It's all in the numbers; Carrera engine No. P90785 originally came in the Porsche Speedster No. A3260, which is currently owned by an enthusiast in Reno. Kane is now trying to reunite his engine with the original Speedster. *Jim Kane*

Mustard sold the Carrera engine to a customer who never picked it up. So it sat in his shop until another customer, Jake Smith, bought it to convert his 1957 Porsche coupe into a Carrera.

The engine sat in a cardboard box in Smith's bedroom, and the Porsche sat in the leaky shed for the next 47 years until purchased by Kane. When Kane saw the engine and spoke to the owner, he decided he needed to own it. He negotiated with Smith and purchased it for $7,500.

"It was a very reasonable price," he said. "I'd say the engine is probably worth about ninety thousand dollars, especially to the guy who owns Speedster No. A3260 today."

Kane began to frequent a couple of Porsche 356 websites and eventually discovered that the car was now owned by Ranson Webster of Reno, Nevada.

"I left a message at his software company that I had the correct engine for his car," said Kane, who noted that Webster's Speedster currently has a Carrera engine, albeit with the wrong serial number.

Initially Webster didn't seem too interested, but he and Kane speak occasionally, and Kane is optimistic that Webster will decide to purchase it.

"A correct, numbers-matching Porsche Speedster is probably worth two hundred fifty thousand dollars these days," he said. "Until it sells, it's just going to remain sitting on the floor in my spare bedroom, where it's not taking up too much room."

And the 1957 Porsche that started it all? "I sold the coupe after I looked into what the car would cost to restore and what it would be worth when finished," said Kane.

Sometimes the parts are worth more than the car.

The Topless
Reunion Cobra

Earl Pfeifer was told about a 289 Cobra by a friend of his who owned a 427 Cobra. His friend wasn't particularly interested in pursuing the car, and the owner wasn't particularly interested in selling it. But one day the friend mentioned the car to Pfeifer, and he went on the prowl.

Pfeifer's father was the new car sales manager at Metro Ford in downtown Calgary, Canada. Back in 1966, his father had met Carroll Shelby in Los Angeles and toured the Shelby plant. As soon as he got back home, he ordered two 1966 Shelby GT350s—one red and one blue—and a 427 Cobra. He kept the red GT350 as his demonstrator. His son Earl has been in love with the brand ever since.

"It was always my dream car," said Pfeifer, 50, who is retired and living in Kalso, British Columbia. "I wanted to buy [the 289 Cobra], even though I heard it was pretty rough."

Earl Pfeifer surveys his new investment, an abused and ignored ex–street race Cobra. CSX2100, the 100th Cobra produced, had been driven hard and put away wet when Pfeifer and his young wife, Carol, sold their brand-new Corvette to buy it. *Earl Pfeifer collection*

The inside of the rat-infested Cobra was a mess, but the Pfeifers restored the car themselves. After rebuilding the bucket seats, they were used in the couple's apartment as living room furniture. *Earl Pfeifer collection*

When he finally was able to see it, rough wasn't the word. "It belonged to a guy who street raced the car," he said. "It had a high-rise manifold, a different carburetor, and 4:56 rear end gears." The engine was also "dolled" up with a Moroso air cleaner and valve covers.

"The guy didn't really care about Cobras, just about speed, so when he seized the engine, he just parked the car and forgot about it," said Pfeifer. "He had the engine all souped up with Chevy valves, but they used the wrong locks and retainers. And the guy who owned the car before him cared even less about it; he parked that thing for years outside in the street."

Carol Pfeifer strikes a provocative pose in the partially restored Cobra. Carol once drove the car topless for 100 miles in order to avoid tan lines, much to the delight of passing truckers. *Earl Pfeifer collection*

But there was one significant thing about this Cobra that got Pfeifer's attention: the serial number was CSX2100, which means it was the 100th Cobra to roll off Carroll Shelby's assembly line. He *needed* to own that car.

So the negotiations began. The owner wanted $40,000 for the car, which was what nice Cobras were selling for at the time. This car was far from nice, but Pfeifer's young wife, Carol, was as into the Cobra purchase as he was. He was 22 years old; she was 20.

"It took about three months, but we finally got him talked down to thirty-two thousand dollars Canadian, which was about twenty-six thousand dollars U.S. at the time," he said.

"We didn't have that kind of money, so we emptied out our small savings account, and I borrowed ten thousand dollars from my father. Then we sold our new 1981 Corvette. As a daily driver, I bought a Chevy Biscayne for twenty dollars. That Cobra left us completely broke and in debt."

When the deal was completed, he inspected the car carefully. Besides the seized engine, the car was loaded with mice. It was also missing lots of the original Cobra components.

"The owner told us that most of the missing parts were probably lying around on the farm," said Pfeifer. "So we spent an entire day searching this guy's property and barns for Cobra parts.

"We found the original soft top buried in the mud under the back steps to his house. I found the original Autolite carburetor and cast-iron manifold sitting sideways on the dirt floor of one of the barns."

The restoration began. Cobra parts were strewn all over the young couple's apartment for three years. The seats were in such poor condition that the Pfeifers peeled the leather covers off the seat frames and treated the leather with conditioner from the inside. When the leather again became pliable, the seats were reassembled, installed on wooden crates and used in the couple's apartment as furniture.

When the car was completed, the couple drove the black roadster with gusto—not just Earl, but Carol too.

"Once we were driving the Cobra back from someplace, and Carol, who was driving, complained to me that because guys could take off their shirts, they never had to worry about tan lines," he said. "So I told her, 'Don't let me stop you.' So she drove the next hundred miles topless, much to the delight of all the truckers, who really liked it; they blasted their horns and gave her the thumbs-up."

Another time Earl was eating lunch with some friends at an outdoor restaurant, where at least 150 people were dining outside. Carol was supposed to meet her own friends at the same restaurant. All of a sudden, there was this big roar, and everyone looked up.

"Carol decided to drive the Cobra, which made quite a bit of noise with the 4:56 gears," he said. "She drove right up to the front of the restaurant, parked the car, and got out. You could have heard a pin drop in that place.

"She was five foot nine inches and one hundred nineteen pounds, so when she drove that Cobra, she got a lot of attention."

Another time, Carol was approached about selling the Cobra. "She came home one day and seemed kind of pissed off," said Pfeifer. "I finally asked her what was bothering her. She handed me a business card that had been left on the car's windshield. On the back of the card was written, 'Dear Sir, if you ever want to sell this car, please call me.'

"I said, 'So?'"

She replied, "Dear Sir?"

Carol stewed about this for about an hour then called the guy who had left the card. "She used a syrupy voice and said she owned the car and was thinking about selling it," said Pfeifer. "She asked the guy if he'd like to go for a ride. Well, off she went and came back an hour later. She took the guy for a ride on a Calgary road called Elbow Drive.

"He didn't buy the car, but she was smiling for the rest of the day."

But all good things must come to an end. With the value of Cobras rising faster than the young Pfeifers' salaries, they sold CSX2100 in 1985 for about $42,000. They were still struggling financially, paying $300 a month for an apartment.

"We were broke, and forty-two thousand dollars was big money to us," he said.

In 1989, Earl and Carol divorced.

"I hadn't talked to her in eighteen years; all I knew was that she lived somewhere in Calgary," he said.

Earl went on to become a successful businessman, owning the franchising rights to the Subway restaurant chain in New Zealand. He opened 140 of the sub shops across the country. But by 2004, he had enough of the food business and sold his company so he could return to Canada.

He was contacted by a friend, who wished to purchase CSX2100 from the current owner and wanted Earl to verify the car's history. When the transaction was completed, Earl got his former wife's email address from his mother and sent her a note with a photo.

"Remember this old car?" he wrote. "Well some guy just paid $540,000 for it!"

That email led to a couple of conversations and a visit by Carol to Earl's home.

"Now we're back together again," he said proudly.

So the guy got the girl, but is he going to try and buy CSX2100 again?

Nope. He currently owns a Boss 429, a 1970 Shelby GT500 SCJ, and 427 Cobra CSX3282.

So it's a happy ending. Although there is no news yet on whether Carol is working on her tans lines again. . . .

Return of the GT350

Pfeifer's father was the sales manager at Metro Ford, and his new-car demonstrator in 1966 was a Shelby GT350.

"I remember being very excited when I was a kid about being able to crawl into the trunk from the back of the car," said Earl Pfeifer.

Eventually a new demonstrator arrived, and the Shelby was sold to a happy customer. Pfeifer's father still had the original invoice, which showed that the base car sold for $3,315, but included options such as chrome wheels ($111.59), rally stripe ($47.50), rear seat ($38), and freight ($141.75), for a total invoice price of $3,653.54 Canadian.

When Bill Pfeifer (back), Earl's dad, was sales manager of Metro Ford in Calgary, his demonstrator was this 1966 Shelby GT350. Pictured with Bill are the three Pfeifer boys. *Left to right:* Mike, Earl, and Gavin. *Earl Pfeifer collection*

The Shelby sold to a bricklayer who used to load up the car with bricks and boards until the rear of the car almost dragged on the ground.

The Pfeifer family all but forgot about the Shelby.

Until 2002.

Pfeifer had kept a copy of the Shelby's VIN and tracked down the car to an owner in Edmonton. Even though he lived in New Zealand at the time, he began communicating with the Shelby's owner, Craig Shanley, and asked if he would consider selling it.

"He said no," said Pfeifer. "He had owned the car for seventeen or eighteen years and had begun a restoration eleven years earlier. The problem was the restoration had stalled and so had the owner's energy to complete it.

"I kept talking to Craig long distance from New Zealand. Finally, after a year or two, he relented and sold me the car.

"I flew back from New Zealand and met my brother in Edmonton to trailer the car home. The car was completely disassembled, and Craig had bolted it back together enough to get it onto the trailer if we picked up the front end."

When father Bill turned 70, his three sons tracked down the very same GT350 and presented it to their father as a birthday present. The grown sons overshadow their father. *Left to right:* Mike, Bill, Earl, and Gavin. *Earl Pfeifer collection*

The brothers brought the car home and presented it to their dad for his 70th birthday.

"The car had had a reasonable life and was ninety-nine percent original," said Pfeifer. "It took dad about a year to reassemble it.

"My dad met the bricklayer who hauled his materials around in the trunk. The guy asked my father if he had to replace the backs of the front seats because of dents.

"My dad said, 'Yes, how did they get there?'

"'Because I used to stack bricks behind the seats and throw two-by-four boards into the car, which dented the seat backs.'"

Shelby in a Snowdrift

When Pfeifer was a 16-year-old, he was working on a 1930 Model A coupe, which he had hoped to make into a hot rod. But he needed an engine.

Hoping to buy a 427-cubic-inch engine for his hot rod Model A Ford, Pfeifer instead bought the engine and the 1967 GT500 it came in. After digging the car out of a snowbank, he brought the car home, restored it, and added much more horsepower. *Earl Pfeifer collection*

"Someone told me about a guy down in Sandpoint, Idaho, who had a 427 Ford engine he would sell," he said. "So a friend and I drove to Sandpoint in the middle of the winter to buy the engine, which was sitting in his garage."

Out of curiosity, the young enthusiast asked what car the engine had been removed from.

"See that lump of snow out there?" asked the owner. "That's my GT500 race car."

With that, the two youths charged out into the bitter cold and through knee-deep snow toward the lump, which turned out to be 1967 GT500 No. 67410F5A00344.

"We uncovered it and asked about buying it," said Pfeifer. "My dad loaned me the money; I think we paid about four thousand five hundred dollars for it.

"At the time, it was illegal to import cars into Canada, so it took my dad and me a couple of years to figure out how to get it done. My dad met an American who was moving to Canada. To make it legal, he purchased the car and brought it into Canada as part of his personal effects.

"We abided by all the laws, but in truth, he never laid eyes on the car."

Pfeifer restored the car as well as a 16-year-old can and rebuilt the engine with aluminum heads and a tunnel-port dual-quad intake manifold. He also

A couple of years later, Pfeifer turned the ex–quarter miler into a very respectable–and fast–street car. The car was equipped with a Cobra 427 Comp engine with nitrous oxide and 3.08 gears; one of his fondest teenage memories is one night spinning the speedometer past 160 miles per hour. *Earl Pfeifer collection*

installed a nitrous-oxide system, which was a new technology at the time.

"But it made the car very fast," he said. "I found out that the engine had originally come out of a 427 Competition Cobra.

"I had 3.08 rear end gears in the car, and I remember one night my brother had the speedometer 'wrapped' [spun beyond zero] to one hundred sixty miles per hour at seven thousand rpm's.

"I was eighteen years old."

CHAPTER EIGHT

The Good, the Bad, and the Lucky

The Good Samaritan
El Camino

By Alan Sangiacomo

I've owned a lot of enjoyable and interesting cars over the years, but the barn-find 1972 El Camino SS I presently own is proof that truth can definitely be stranger than fiction.

In the spring of 2005, I decided I wanted a muscle car. Because I have a disability that necessitates using a wheelchair, I figured my options were limited. As I've gotten older, the injury has forced me to limit my search to cars that I can actually get into! "Maybe an El Camino, or something similar, where I could install a wheelchair lift in the bed," I thought.

With this in mind, I started casually looking and putting the word out to friends. I started to pick up car magazines and *Auto Trader* guides at the supermarket to see what was out there. I watched the car ads and kept my eyes open. I even went to see a 1967 or 1968 El Camino about 40 miles away from my Albany, New York, home that the seller—who wanted a small fortune for the car—said "just needed a little work" to put it into top shape. When I arrived to see the car, the junker was buried up to the axles in a muddy field and hadn't been started in at least 10 years. The interior was home to something furry, and no body panel lacked serious rust. Needless to say, I took a pass on the car.

It seemed that everything I came across was in one of three categories: too expensive, a total basket case ready for the scrap heap, or a badly done, nonoriginal re-creation with no pedigree.

I had about given up my muscle car quest when I received a call from a friend who told me to check out an ad he saw in a supermarket car ad magazine. "1971 SS El Camino, fully restored, multiple award winner, handicapped accessible."

I figured what the heck, and I called. The elderly lady who answered was very nice, and she proceeded to tell me her story. The car was presently in Arkansas, and it had been owned by her late son since 2001. The car had been originally built in Kansas City and remained in that part of the country all its life. It was actually a 1972 car, not a 1971 as incorrectly advertised. She was selling the El Camino because her son had passed away suddenly the previous autumn. The car had been in storage since.

She said the car was in very good condition when her son bought it, but it still needed work. He had wanted to restore it to showroom condition. And because he had a disability that necessitated a wheelchair, he wanted to make

232

When Alan Sangiacomo was searching for a collector car that could haul his wheelchair, he never believed he'd actually find one that had a wheelchair hoist already installed! This 1972 SS El Camino was purchased from the mother of a deceased wheelchair-bound son. The mother wanted Sangiacomo to own it next. *Alan Sangiacomo*

the El Camino handicap-accessible in the process. She said the car was a source of pride and joy for her son and its restoration a labor of love. Over the next couple of years, he brought the car to shows, and as he saved up additional money, he would continue improving the car.

At some point early in our conversation, I told her about my disability and my search for the right car that could haul my wheelchair. It seemed the more we talked, the more similarities we found between her son's life and mine. She was asking for a lot of money for the car, which I told her up-front was out of my price range, but she said she'd send me some pictures, background information, and records, and we could talk more if I was still interested.

The material she sent me was a treasure-trove. I had a copy of the bill of sale to her son and a history of the car. She sent me pictures of how it looked when her son acquired it, pictures of various stages of its restoration, and documentation of all sorts. It had, indeed, won several trophies and was even featured in a local car magazine. The most recent restoration had taken her son's mechanic friend 10 months and included a complete restoration of the paint, interior, and engine, as well as mounting a remote-actuated wheelchair lift in the pickup bed.

Her son suddenly collapsed and died two weeks after getting the car back from restoration.

After reviewing the documentation and talking to the mechanic who had done all the work, I called the woman again. Over the next month or so we became friends as we chatted often about the car, her son, and disability issues. Even though I desperately wanted the car, I had to be honest with her; I could only afford to give her less than half of what she was asking, and I understood if she had the opportunity to sell it to someone else for more. However, she called me the next day and said she talked to her pastor. "We talked about you and my son and we prayed on it," she told me. "And, I think my son would want you to have this car!"

She sold the El Camino to me for a price I could afford and agreed to allow me to have it transported to my mechanic secured with a 50 percent deposit and the balance due after his inspection. She even threw in the trophies the car had won and a car cover. Her final words to me were simply, "You're getting a heck of a deal."

Once I had the car shipped to my mechanic, we found lots of work that still needed to be done. The engine had to be dismantled down to the bare block, then reassembled with new high-performance parts and a remote starter switch. The 12-bolt rear end was new, as was the interior, air conditioning equipment, and flawless paint job. And, the wheelchair lift was perfectly matched to my needs.

I've done lots more work since. The transmission had to be rebuilt; I installed new outside mirrors, along with other trim; and the underside mechanicals, suspension, gas tank, and steering box are all new. There's still a little more work to be done, but that will have to wait until time and finances allow.

So, that's my twist on a barn-find story. Right now, I'm bringing the car to shows, cruising, and just generally having a blast. All thanks to a friend, a spur-of-the-moment phone call, and the generosity of a special person.

Bad Luck Blues

The call was routine; Cliff Bieder and his partner William Heiser received word from Homeland Security that the agency had just discovered a car that had been listed as stolen.

Bieder and Heiser were New York City cops working in the Organized Crime Buereau, Auto Theft Division. This case was right up their alley; most of the auto theft crimes they responded to had to do with VIN numbers being switched or stolen cars that were being shipped out of the country.

But this case had a twist; the car had been stolen 37 years earlier.

"I was always a car guy, so when I found a home in the police department that involved cars, I stayed," said Bieder, now 49, who was in the department for 25 years before retiring.

The case intrigued the two officers, first of all because it was a 1968 Corvette, and second because it had disappeared nearly four decades earlier, when the car was almost new.

On January 22, 1969, a blue-on-blue Corvette was stolen from Alan Poster, capping off the worst year of his life. The 26-year-old guitar salesman from Brooklyn had just gotten a divorce, so he treated himself to a $6,000 present he could barely afford: a nearly new Corvette. And he moved into his own apartment on 23rd Street in Manhattan. He was so short on cash after the purchase that he couldn't afford the theft coverage on his insurance policy.

"I went out on the limb to get this thing," Poster, now 67, told the *New York Times* in 2006. "It was an egocentric muscle car that just came out. Back then, the Corvette was hot as heck and an absolute fantasy of mine."

Poster kept the Corvette in a parking garage, but on that January day, when the parking attendant went to retrieve the car, he returned and informed him the car was missing. He had owned the car for only two-and-a-half months.

After filing a police report, Poster was given little hope of ever seeing his beloved blue Corvette again. Police were busy that January; only 22 days into the new year and already 6,620 cars had been reported stolen in New York City. By year's end, the number would exceed 78,000.

So Poster chalked the loss up to his continuing streak of bad luck, packed his bags, and moved to San Francisco to start a business building cases for cameras, guitars, and drums. His $6,000 investment and the car were history.

Thirty-seven long years passed, with Poster never really giving the Corvette another thought. The car resurfaced when a Swedish collector paid $10,000 for the car. Where the car had been is unclear. What is clear is that the car's original 350-cubic-inch small-block had been substituted for a

This is how officers Cliff Bieder and William Heiser found Alan Poster's 1968 Corvette as it was about to leave the United States in a container bound for Sweden. Painted silver with red interior, it was a far cry from the blue-on-blue Corvette that was stolen from Poster in 1969. *Alan Poster collection*

Lights, camera, action! In 2006, Poster (center) sees the Corvette for the first time since it was stolen from him 37 years earlier. The reunion became a huge media event for Poster and officers Bieder and Heiser. *Alan Poster collection*

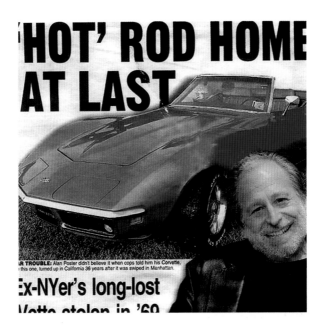

'HOT' ROD HOME AT LAST

R TROUBLE: Alan Poster didn't believe it when cops told him his Corvette, this one, turned up in California 36 years after it was swiped in Manhattan.

Ex-NYer's long-lost Vette stolen in '69

The saga of Poster's Corvette was documented by the *New York Times.* Poster became a successful businessman in San Francisco. *Alan Poster collection*

454 big-block. And what had been a blue Corvette with blue interior was now silver with red interior. For some reason, the transmission and gas tank were missing.

Bieder and Heiser were informed of the pending sale of a potentially stolen vehicle to the collector.

"We got this call from Homeland Security that they had this car that had been stolen in 1969," said Bieder. "They found it during a numbers check as it was being loaded onto a boat for Sweden.

"Because the car was stolen in the days before computers, we had our work cut out for us."

The two officers went to police headquarters in Lower Manhattan and searched through thousands of records on microfilm files. They were working under a tight deadline, because if Bieder and Heiser couldn't find the records within just a few days, the car would be shipped to Sweden. But on the second day, they struck gold; they secured a report of a Mr. Poster whose Corvette was stolen in 1969.

Bieder and Heiser had a friendly bet going with another officer who said they'd never find the theft report before the January 1 deadline. Bieder remembers a nice steak dinner was the payoff, which he and Heiser enjoyed at their colleague's expense.

Finding Poster, though, proved to be a chore. They checked at various addresses in the New York metropolitan area without luck. But a resident of a house in New Jersey that Poster sold him said he thought Poster moved to California.

"Is this some kind of a joke?" asked Poster when he was notified by Bieder that his Corvette had been found. "I never thought I'd see that car again."

Since reclaiming his Corvette in 2006, Poster has had the car completely restored back to its blue-on-blue color scheme. Following the restoration, the car was displayed at the huge Corvette show in Carlisle, Pennsylvania.

"And we got a call from Diane Sawyer to appear on *Good Morning America*," said Bieder. The two officers became instant celebrities and appeared on CNN, in the *New York Times*, and in other media outlets.

"Things don't happen by accident," said Poster in the 2006 *New York Times* article. "Things come back to me; I have no idea why. Maybe it all comes back to you at some point."

Pikeville Purgatory

What would happen if a car dealership closed, just closed, and sat untouched for three decades?

In the showroom, brochure racks would still be filled with colorful materials showing the latest models, body styles, and colors for cars that were new when Jimmy Carter was in the White House. The parts department would still be stocked with water pumps, distributor caps and brake shoes. And, of course, there would be row upon row of used cars out on the lot.

Welcome to Collier Motors in the tiny, rural town Pikeville, North Carolina. Owner Robert Collier is the third-generation owner of a dealership that was begun by his grandfather more than 100 years ago. His grandfather opened the dealership early in the last century as an outlet for Whippet, Studebaker, and Willys Overland vehicles. Collier's father converted the dealership to sell and service Nash and Rambler automobiles, which Robert Collier took over and owns to this day.

Hundreds of vehicles pass by the former dealership every day, the occupants never knowing what relics reside behind the metal fence and dense vegetation. Yet a walk of less than 50 feet through those trees reveals a strange combination of a time-capsule car dealership and Jurassic Park.

A once-thriving AMC dealership in North Carolina was suddenly closed down in the 1970s. It remains a time capsule today, although overgrown with trees and weeds, which have taken over the parking area and used car lot. *Tom Cotter*

Robert Collier inside the once stylish showroom of Collier Motors in Pikeville, North Carolina, which now sits forlorn and neglected. It contains two rare AMX two-seaters, a Packard sedan, an Ambassador convertible, and a few motorcycles. Roof leaks have caused the ceiling tiles to fall down on the cars. *Tom Cotter*

"I was a Rambler and American Motors dealership since the 1950s," said Robert Collier, 80, who along with his son Rob, still operates the former dealership. "But when American Motors was purchased by the French, I just closed down.

"I wasn't going to sell none of them Renaults."

American Motors Corporation was partially purchased by the French-owned Renault company in 1979.

He installed an eight-foot-tall cyclone fence around the property and locked the gate, but continues to fiddle with his Ramblers to this day. Initially his old customers brought their Ramblers for him to repair, but as those cars got older and were taken off the road, his business declined.

He continued to work on his Matadors, Rebels, Marlins, and Javelins, but father and son also started to collect significant American Motors automobiles. They began to search out and purchase the rare two-seater AMX muscle cars. Today the Colliers probably own a dozen examples, including two very low mileage examples in excellent condition that are still sitting in the one-time showroom. Others are rusting and rotting into the ground.

Probably the most interesting AMX in the Collier collection once belonged to the late Arizona senator Barry Goldwater. According to Collier,

What was once a used car lot is now overgrown and nearly impassable. More than 250 cars are still parked in rows on the property, but many—especially the convertibles—have trees growing right through the body! *Tom Cotter*

The Colliers have several Nash-Healey sports cars, two coupes and two convertibles. This one, believe it or not, is said to have won its class at the Pebble Beach Concours decades ago. Now it sits rotting into the earth. When asked if he would consider selling one, Mr. Collier said yes, but these days "they sell for at least two hundred thousand dollars." *Tom Cotter*

One of the few celebrity-owned cars is this 1969 AMX, which was purchased new by Arizona senator Barry Goldwater. The Colliers purchased the car from the senator's estate, but unfortunately have kept it outdoors ever since, so it has rapidly deteriorated. *Tom Cotter*

Goldwater bought the bright red coupe new for about $5,000, "But he invested at least another hundred thousand dollars in accessories and special equipment," he said.

Goldwater had a number of hobbies—ham radio, American Indian kachina dolls, photography, and UFO studies—but he also was a car buff and enjoyed modifying his AMX.

Likely through his government and armed services connections, Goldwater had several aircraft gauges installed in the dashboard, including an altimeter. He also installed Recaro driving seats and a custom steering wheel.

Displayed across the trunk deck are decals signifying all the states he had driven his AMX through during his ownership. He apparently also drove the car throughout Europe, which was documented in a three-page summary in his autobiography. Also displayed on the car's rear license tag was his ham radio frequency number.

When Goldwater died in 1998, Collier contacted the family about purchasing the senator's car. After a short negotiation, a deal was finalized with Goldwater's son.

That's the good news. The bad news is that since the desirable AMX has been transported from the arid Arizona climate to the humidity of North

Carolina, it has been sitting outside in a back lot at Collier's facility and has begun rusting away.

Parked randomly throughout the property are a number of Javelins, including several Mark Donohue editions that commemorated his winning of the 1971 SCCA Trans-Am Championship.

Collier said he has at least 250 used cars still parked on his property. Although they were once probably parked on gravel or grass, after 30 years of not cutting the lawn, those cars are now parked in a mature forest. All sorts of AMC sedans, station wagons, and convertibles (some with trees actually growing through the fabric roof) are littered in rows throughout the several-acre lot. However, the used car lot is not only comprised of AMC products, but also random brands such as Chevrolets, Fords, Chryslers, Cadillacs, and even Mercedes-Benzes.

"I think I have about two hundred fifty cars in the lot, but I'd have to count the titles to be sure," said Collier. With all the trees and plant growth around the cars, it more resembles a metallic jungle than a proper car lot.

Probably the most valuable single cars on the property are the collection of Nash-Healeys that the Colliers have assembled. Nash-Healey sports cars were manufactured between 1951 and 1954 and created out of a partnership between the Nash Motor Company—the American company, which supplied the special multi-carb high-performance engine and drivetrain—and Donald Healey—the British sports car builder who supplied the chassis, suspension, and technical expertise. The two-seater bodies were manufactured in Italy.

The cars were an odd combination of components that seemed to work better than anyone imagined. The cars performed well on the racetrack and finished as high as third place at the 24 Hours of Le Mans in 1952. But because components for the car came from three places—Nash in Kenosha, Wisconsin, Healey in Warwick, England, and the bodies from Turin, Italy—the cars were expensive for the day. The cars cost nearly $6,500, which in the early 1950s made it one of the most expensive sports car of the day.

Only 507 cars were built over its three-year production life. But the car has a loyal following among collectors today. The renowned Walnut Creek, California, car collector, the late Jacques "Frenchy" Harguindeguy, who owned a fleet of classics including the Best in Show Pebble Beach 1936 Delehaye roadster, considered his Nash-Healey one of the best cars ever built and chose to drive it over all his other priceless cars.

The Colliers have four Nash-Healeys scattered around the former dealer-ship. The good news is that two of the rare cars are parked in what was formerly the service department. The bad news is that the other two are parked outside in the elements.

One particularly disturbing example is a Nash-Healey Le Mans Coupe, a stylish hardtop that was built to commemorate the brand's racing successes.

When I walked up to Collier's coupe, the door was ajar and the outside was indeed inside. Moss, mold, and other organic materials were equally spread on both the outside and inside of this once magnificent car. The car's once red and black body was totally covered in rust, and cancer had become firmly entrenched within the car's extremities.

What I couldn't believe was what Collier said next.

"We bought that car on the West Coast right after it won at Pebble Beach," he said. I was dumbstruck. This rusted hulk, which if restored would require a truckload of money and years of time, had been a gleaming, polished, and perfect example once displayed at the most revered Concours d'Elegance in the world.

Out of respect for the car's history, I walked back to the Nash-Healey and pushed the door shut. But it sprung back open.

Robert Collier is an interesting fellow. He was obviously a competent businessman who ran the family dealership in the 1950s when he was in his 20s; he is mechanically astute, and he knows the value of vintage cars and parts. But he seems to have no sense of preservation. He owns significant cars, but instead of protecting the cars, and therefore his investments, they are put out to pasture where their conditions rapidly deteriorate.

Hoping to save some of the cars, I asked if any were for sale.

"Sure, everything is for sale," he said.

I asked about the Nash-Healey Le Mans Coupe, which had been rusting terribly outside for decades.

"Yup, I'll sell it."

"How much are you asking," I asked.

"Well," he said, "I'd have to think about that. But that car won at Pebble Beach, and they sell for at least two hundred thousand dollars."

There was nothing left for me to say. I shook his hand and thanked him for allowing me to see his facility. I've been haunted about the dilemma of his cars ever since.

And at this very moment, all of them are still sitting there, rusting into the ground.

The Ratso Rizzo
Giulietta

Jim Barrett didn't start out life as an Alfa guy, although he was certainly an alpha male. You see, back as a kid, like so many American car guys, he fell in love with Carroll Shelby's AC Cobras. But Barrett carried his love affair too far and actually bought one.

In 1973, he chased down an ad for a 289 Cobra, CSX2533, one of the last of the small-block series. And he bought it. It was a decent, original car in British Racing Green. The price was $6,000, and the good news is that he still owns the car today. But we're not here to talk about Cobras, we're here to talk about Alfas.

In 1990 Barrett's wife, Elyse, took the job as editor of *Alfa Owner* magazine, a position she held for three-and-a-half years. During that time the couple became exposed to a car that they lucked into and would become infatuated with—their 1957 Giulietta 750 Sprint.

"The friend of a former friend's father died and had this old Alfa in his garage," said Barrett, 62, of Huntington Beach, California. "The family wanted to liquidate the father's assets, so a local Costa Mesa Alfa mechanic made a real low-ball offer of one thousand dollars. The family was insulted and just offered it to my friend and me for free. 'You can just have it,' they said. We owned it fifty-fifty."

By this time the Alfa was sitting outside in the driveway of a neighbor who had agreed to store it for the family. Barrett and his friend went to retrieve the car the following Saturday, but the neighbor who had stored it didn't want to let them have it.

"The guy, who was a car guy himself, didn't believe that we were given the car for free," said Barrett. "I went ballistic! I knew we had to act fast, because every other Alfa guy in the area was bound to find out about it and try to get it themselves.

"We tried to call the son who gave us the car, but we couldn't get hold of him. I was going to puke; I just knew we were going to lose the car."

Finally Barrett convinced the neighbor that he was a good, upstanding citizen and gave him his address and phone number in case there was any discrepancy to the story.

They loaded the rare little coupe onto a trailer and drove back to Jim's house to do inventory. It had been a typical restoration project gone bad: the transmission was in the trunk; the engine was resting on the rear package shelf; and there were various engine parts, such as valve seals, main bearings, and rod bearings,

Beside owning a bitchin' old 289 Cobra, Jim and Elyse Barrett are Alfa Romeo aficionados. Through a friend, they followed a lead on a long-neglected 1957 Giulietta 750 Sprint that was sitting in a Southern California yard. The car's body was sound, but otherwise it was pretty raunchy. *Jim Barrett*

scattered throughout the interior of the car. Also, in the rear cargo area was a spare back window glass, which for a coupe was a rare find. And he found a dead rat. Unfortunately, they never did find the correct front seats or the radiator.

"But the ignition key was still in the ignition switch, and the California black plates were still screwed on the car," said Barrett.

They dragged the car home in 2005. Since that time, the two friends have had a permanent falling-out, so Barrett wound up owning 100 percent of the Alfa.

So the dilemma for Barrett is this: What to do with this car?

He has come up with three scenarios on the direction to take this car once his other projects are completed:

Choice No. 1—A proper rotisserie restoration. Barrett is friendly with Freeman Thomas, head designer at Ford Motor Company, and J. Mays, designer of the new VW Beetle, Audi TT, and Ford Flex. Thomas has recommended that if Barrett takes this direction, the car would look best in dark blue paint with either gray or brown leather interior. Barrett figures this approach would require a $40,000 investment.

When they got their new acquisition home, Jim and Elyse (pictured) removed everything from the car, including taking the engine out of the back seat area and the transmission from the trunk. *Jim Barrett*

Choice No. 2—Beater. "This is where I put the car together as-is, get it running, and drive the piss out of it," he said. He doesn't know the exact expenses yet, but admits this would be the most reasonably priced direction to go.

Choice No. 3—Rat rod! Barrett gets the most excited about this option, and it actually seems most appropriate because of the dead rat he discovered when cleaning out the car. "I'd paint it flat gray primer with ghost flames in multiple shades of purple," he said. "But like all good rat rods, even though the body of the car may look like a rat, the wheels and tires would need to be bitchin', so I'd probably install new Boranni wheels." He further dreams about pitching the original 1300cc engine, which produced about 65 horsepower, and instead installing a souped-up 2-liter with polished Weber carburetors and velocity stacks and white-coated headers. "Or what would be really cool would be to find one of the old Autodelta twin-plug racing engines that they used to race in the under 2.5-liter Trans-Am in the early 1970s," he said. "I'd probably run a straight-pipe exhaust and install GTV6 seats, which have thin shells, and upholster them in black with red piping. I'd install a beer cooler below the back luggage shelf that could drain out onto the ground. And I'd have to

One of the Barrett's favorite automotive helpers is Henry Nichols, the five-year-old neighbor boy. At the pace Barrett is working on the Alfa, Henry may graduate from college before it is completed. *Jim Barrett*

install a Momo steering wheel and some kind of Boyd Coddington–type billet aluminum rear-view mirror." Clearly, he has thought this direction out to the finest details. Barrett figures this conversion would cost somewhere in the area of $10,000 to $15,000 to produce.

But until he decides which way to turn with his Alfa Giulietta coupe project, it will continue to sit in his driveway, blocking the garage door that houses his Cobra.

Appendix

Eleven More Barn-Finding Tips

In *The Hemi in the Barn*, I listed 20 barn-finding tips that I've developed since I was a kid riding my bicycle to look for old cars. Since that book was published, I've heard from you with some of your favorite suggestions for unearthing old rust buckets. So, here are your 11 favorite suggestions for discovering automotive artifacts:

1. Lawyers are a Barn-Finder's Best Friend

Make friends with local lawyers, who may know about estates that are being settled due to bankruptcy, death, or whatever. You never know, something interesting just might be lurking in that old garage out back.

2. Check Out Estate Auction Websites

Lately, the contents of more and more estate auctions are being listed on the Internet. Sometimes, listed between the porcelain doll collection and the wooden kitchen cabinet, there might be a Maserati. . . .

3. Tree Surgeons Do it Up High

A tree surgeon at the Hot Rod Reunion in Bakersfield, California, told me he gets a great view into people's backyards and behind fences when he's climbing and trimming branches in residential neighborhoods.

4. Business Cards

Have business cards printed that urge people to call you if they want to sell their car and leave them under the windshield wipers of interesting cars in the parking lot.

5. Go Postal

Mail carriers know the every crack in the sidewalks of the neighborhoods they service, especially if they walk their mail routes. The mail carriers know who reads what magazines on their routes and just might know what is resting behind the backyard fence.

6. Mechanic Liens

Check with local repair shops, especially shops that might service specialty cars such as Porsches or antique cars. These shops are often "stuck" with unfinished restoration projects because owners can't afford to pay the balance of their invoices. Often these cars can be purchased for the payment of past services or at a small auction.

7. DMV

Make friends with someone in your local Department of Motor Vehicles, or possibly a policeman, who can legally run VIN checks on long-forgotten cars that may have been removed from the road.

8. We Buy Junk Cars

Have you ever seen those ads or signs on the side of the road? Just who are these people and where do the cars go? Well, it turns out that often car towing companies are asked to remove relics from people's yards or garages. True "junk" is taken directly to the crusher, but cars in better condition are often taken to the towing yard for storage until a buyer can be found.

9. Seek Out Old Collectors

My friend Jim Maxwell and I recently hit the road early on an 11-degree, snowy morning (brains are not mandatory), promising not to return home until we found something cool. Well, toward the end of the day, we met a number of older collectors who at one time had collected and restored older Fords and Mustangs. These days, though, they were not too interested anymore, but still

APPENDIX

owned some cars and parts. It makes me wonder how many ex-collectors live around the United States....

10. Look into the Crystal Ball

Hire a psychic! Who knows, maybe a mind-reader can tell you what is sitting behind the barn door. It sure beats trying to make those comic book x-ray glasses work....

11. Get Your Own Show

Jay Leno has the best platform to seek out old cars. One old-car mention during his television show has the phone in his Burbank office ringing off the hook the next morning. If it's not too late, you might want to go back to acting school or practice your stand-up comedy.

Index

252

INDEX